Memories

of

Woking

The publishers would like to thank the following companies for their support in the production of this book

BBF Fielding

Greenfield School

Harpers Group

Herbert Parnell

Unwin Printers

James Walker Group

Woking News and Mail

Woking Review

First published in Great Britain by True North Books Limited
England HX5 9AE
Telephone: 01422 377977

ISBN 1 903204 32 1

Text, design and origination by True North Books Limited
Printed and bound by The Amadeus Press Limited

Memories

of

Woking

Including pictures from

Woking News & Mail Series and Woking Review

Contents

Introduction

Woking has long been known as a thriving commuter town for London. But the town has far more than its position on the railway line to commend it, as those who live here know well, and this new collection of nostalgic images calls to mind the way we once lived in the Woking of our youth.

We revisit the vanished places of entertainment such as the Ritz, where we were once members of the ABC Minors; the Odeon - the scene, perhaps, of our first date? - and the long-gone Grand Theatre, where our parents and grandparents paid 1/6d to see the variety shows. We take a peep back through time at some of the town's notable occasions such as Empire Day, once a red letter day in the school calendar; those happy parties when we celebrated VE Day at the end of World War II; and the wonderful coronation celebrations back in 1953.

We take a trip down Memory Lane and take a look at the good times, when the Rolling Stones visited the Atalanta Ballroom, and those long, hot sunny days when we cooled off at the Woking Lido. We go on a shopping spree around stores such as Robinson's, Gammons, and Skeet & Jeffes, which were destined to go out of business or vanish below modern shopping complexes, and we thrill again to the science fiction stories of H G Wells, who put Woking firmly on the map (and destroyed it again!) in his novel 'The War of the Worlds'.

Continued overleaf

From previous page
There were, of course, the not so good times, when the people of Woking squared their shoulders and simply got on with life in the long ago days of air raid shelters, make do and mend, and ration books. And the thankfully long gone days when Brookwood Hospital (known at the time as the Lunatic Asylum) hid their patients away from the public gaze in cold and bleak surroundings.

The 1970s were years when redevelopment brought sweeping changes to Woking; some were warmly welcomed, while others left us with ugly, angular buildings which many saw as a blot on the landscape. Henry Ford was fond of telling his friends, 'Plan for the future, because that's where you're going to spend the rest of your life', and the planning committees of more recent years have acquired the perfect vision of 20/20 hindsight, and

interesting and attractive red brick buildings have made Woking a more pleasant place in which to live. Progress has given us the Peacocks shopping centre, with its tasteful shops and cafes, the Wolsey Place shopping complex, the excellent central library, the marvellous Surrey History Centre, and much, much more. We are fortunate indeed that the 20th Century was so well chronicled, and we have only to compare our present town, with its exciting developments in sport and leisure, commerce and the arts, with Woking as it was, say in the 1950s, to see what progress has been realised and what achievements have been made over the last 50 or so years. Woking has a history we can all be proud of - and just as importantly, a great future to look forward to. We hope that you will read and enjoy 'Memories of Woking' - and remember that history is still in the making.

Street scenes

Back in 1954 Chertsey Road had a wide variety of shops and businesses to tempt passers by to part with their cash. Vegetarians were rare in the 1950s, and Robert Wasley's butcher's shop on the left was an important port of call for the housewives of the day. Sadly, many of our smaller butchers have disappeared, along with the personal service we once took for granted. Small grocery chains and corner butchers were the traditional way to shop, and customers would queue to be served while the butcher cubed our stewing steak and cut our sausages from a long string hanging over the counter. A far cry from today's plastic packs! W A Elton advertised himself as a bookseller, librarian, stationer and printer; the shop was all these things and more, as this was where artists would go to stock up on paint, brushes, pencils and all the other paraphernalia connected with their hobby. Further along was W E Mallard, gents' outfitters, and Pearks' grocery stores where the delivery vehicle is standing. On the right we can pick out the sign outside the Scotch Wool and hosiery stores; all the shops in this block disappeared and were replaced by the Big Apple.

Below: This scene dates from soon before the outbreak of the second world war. ARP volunteers are busy on Chobham Road outside the premises of the Woking Electric Supply Co. There was considerable uncertainty in the months before war broke out and in the early stages of the conflict. the biggest fear was that of an enemy attack from the air. Memories of the devastating gas campaigns in the trenches during the Great War only a generation earlier were fresh in peoples' minds. As a precaution gas masks were issued to every man, woman and child in the UK. In 1939 one and a half million children were evacuated from towns, cities and industrial targets and removed to rural and remote areas considered to be less attractive to enemy bombers. Anti gas squads were formed and trained in every local area and people were encouraged to know the signs of a gas attack in a major campaign of public education. In the event, however, there was never any gas attack on British soil. Locally, as nationally, the ARP spear-

headed attempts to protect the public from the risk of enemy bombing. The main weapon in their armoury was *the blackout* which was designed to conceal the where-abouts of major conurbations. White lines were painted on kerbs, lampposts, car mudguards and telegraph poles to make it easier for people to get around in the darkness. Many injuries were caused as people groped their way around and hundreds of people were prosecuted each week for flouting the blackout regulations.

Bottom: A view to jog our memory and bring to mind a multitude of familiar names which once traded in Chertsey Road. Tyler & Co; Lasletts Linens, the Midland Bank, Central Stores, Glosters Corn Merchants - they were all there, and many more, with Burton's menswear on the corner in the distance. And about half way along on the right stood the old Post Office, which was eventually relocated to

Commercial Road (Commercial Way today). So many changes - yet many readers will remember the way Chertsey Road was in the early 1950s. The cars parked along the left kerbside are typical of the period. By 1953 changes in car design were imminent. Mudguards and running boards like those on the Morris Minor and cars from earlier decades were set to become a thing of the past; headlights would be faired-in and incorporated into sleeker body lines, flashing indicators would replace the semaphore type (remember how easy it was to forget them and leave them sticking out?), and even quarter-light windows would gradually disappear from our cars.

What a marvellous old photograph; it really takes you back, doesn't it? It is a great pity that we have no date for this view of the Chertsey Road and Commercial Road junction, but as pedestrian crossings marked out by studs and yellow beacons were introduced in 1934, and crossings were given their zebra stripes in 1951, this has to be somewhere in between, we would guess at the late 1940s. Those very first 1930s beacons were unwisely made of glass, and when too many of them were broken by little boys with stones the globes were replaced by painted aluminium ones. The year 1952 saw yet more changes when plastic winking globes were introduced. The railing around the gents in the centre of the road was obviously a popular place to park your bike; did anyone ever take home the wrong one by (genuine) mistake? The view includes an unusual number of little boys; were they on their way home after watching Laurel and Hardy at the Plaza, we wonder? We will never know.

aken in, we believe, 1953, this snapshot of Chertsey Road from its junction with Duke Street has something of a 'villagey' atmosphere about it, perhaps partly due to the cluster of cyclists who have stopped for a chat on the corner, and the absence of motorised traffic. A few decades later, a stroll along this end of Chertsey Road would create a very different impression, especially at night when Weatherspoons on the left and the Big Apple indoor entertainment centre, on the right, are both in full swing.

However, dances and celebrations were very much in the air on this day in 1953. The flags are out in honour of the coronation of Queen Elizabeth II,

nd the group on the corner may well be iscussing one or another of the many coronation vents that were scheduled in and around Woking balls, parties, all manner of displays and competiions, civic and religious services, and many more esides. No doubt Woolworths will have a good election of coronation souvenirs on sale; how many readers still have 1953 coronation mugs, teaspoons or biscuit tins, we wonder, or even one of the many coronation picture books which little girls, in particular, loved looking at. And many will remember those flickery, black-and-white TV images of the 1953 coronation as their first ever experience of watching telly.

Bottom: The Gaumont Cinema in Chertsey Road gave Woking many happy hours of enjoyment. There was a cinema on this site as far back as 1912; the first in the town to be purpose-built to show films. It was known as the Central Halls Cinema, although most locals knew it and its immediate successor rather unkindly as the 'fleapit'. In 1927 it was taken over by Frederick Iverson (who at one time also owned the Palace Cinema in Duke Street). Iverson had the cinema rebuilt as the Plaza - which later became the Gaumont. In the late 1950s it fell victim to the red pen of the town planner, and along with surrounding buildings, including the popular Sunray restaurant, it was demolished to make way for a modern shopping centre. Few people were about in Chertsey Road at the time of the photograph; where have all the cyclists gone? The sight of dozens of cycles lined up against the kerb was a regular sight in the town centre, bringing complaints from motorists and pedestrians alike. But those were the days when you could safely leave your bike and go off shopping, and expect to still find it there when you got back! Maxwells Music Shop can be seen on the left of the photograph, with the offices of the Woking News and Mail nearby.

Right: Now Albion House stands on this spot, but generations of townsfolk in times gone by knew this corner as the site of the Albion Hotel. The hotel was in existence for well over a century, during which time it had two different buildings. Reuben Percy, the landlord of the Wheatsheaf Hotel at Horsell, built the first one in 1856-57. Its location proved to be extremely well-chosen; not only was it convenient for the early rail travellers, but when, over the course of the following decades, the new town of Woking grew up around the railway station, the hotel found itself on a prime site. In fact, the Albion Hotel could claim the distinction of having been the first building in the town centre. The 19th century premises were pulled down in 1899 and replaced by the late-Victorian building seen in our picture. In the second half of the 20th century, grand-scale redevelopment of the town centre meant that this key site was no longer the place for a humble Victorian hotel, and in 1965 it was demolished to make way for the Norwich Union's half-million pound office block. This photograph, taken around 1960, shows the familiar view of the Albion Hotel which used to greet people as they emerged from Barclays Bank and faced west.

the new church was laid in 1887; in 1893 Christ Church was consecrated and a new parish was created, comprised of some 4,000 parishioners. More than a hundred years on, the church - now with a coffee shop and bookshop - continues to provide a Christian presence in the town centre.

Top: A tranquil scene from the 1950s featuring a solitary cyclist making his way along Connaught Road at Brookwood. The pace of life seemed much slower in the days depicted here! Some of the shops visible in the photograph are certain to evoke fond memories among people who shopped here or were familiar with this location at the time. Gowns and underwear were the main stock in trade at De-Crecy's, the first shop on the left of the photograph. Further along the street the local Post Office could (and still can) be found, and between them stood the Connaught Cafe, notable here for its acutely angled gable. At the time this picture was taken Britain was still in the process of recovering from the turmoil caused by the second world war. It had, of course, only ended a decade earlier and it took time for our emotional and economic recovery to take place. The 1950s did see a recovery in our fortunes with low unemployment and rising household incomes. By 1957 Harold Macmillan boldly told the public that *they'd never had it so good*. His words would come back to haunt him from time to time but as the 1950s came to a close many Woking people would find it hard to disagree with them.

Above: Christ Church is instantly recognisable, but how different its environs were in 1953! Then, the spire towered high above the surrounding buildings. In the second half of the 20th century, a forest of high-rise office blocks was to spring up all around it: Crown House, Albion House, Export House, Costain House (now Alexander House), and Dukes Court. The Victorian church is the only building in this part of Woking which was not pulled down in the redevelopment programme that commenced towards the end of the 1960s. A century earlier, the former 'new town' of Woking was being created around the railway station, and it was to serve the growing population of this area that the church was built. For many years prior to its construction, services had been held in makeshift accommodation - the back room of a shop, then a temporary iron chapel which by 1885 was cramped, rusty and leaking. The foundation stone for

Robinsons' clock tells us that it is 9am, and Chertsey Road is buzzing with life and activity. On the right, a delivery wagon is off-loading the day's supply of good things to MacFisheries. The popular fish shop was established in 1921 as part of Lord Leverhulme's project to alleviate the plight of Scottish crofters living in poverty. He purchased 300 shops for the express purpose of selling fish, and encouraged crofters to change their calling from the land to the sea. The crofters turned fishermen ensured a regular supply to Lord Leverhulme's shops - and everyone was

happy. A real success story! Passers by who paused to raise their eyes above shop window level would not have failed to notice the large banner above their heads promoting a Cheshire Homes gift shop. Leonard Cheshire founded his first Cheshire Foundation Home for the Incurably Sick in 1948.

Famous for his World War II exploits, Cheshire was awarded the Victoria Cross, Distinguished Service Order with two bars, and Distinguished Flying Cross. What a man! He married Susan Ryder - another familiar personality whose name is linked with helping the sick and disabled - in 1959.

Younger readers may find little that is familiar about this view. The photograph was in fact taken from an upstairs window in Chertsey Road, looking straight down Chobham Road in the days when Chobham Road actually went to Chobham. Across Commercial Road, the drapers shop on the left was Gammons, and that corner was known for many a year as Gammons Corner. In consequence of the radical measures which were taken to rejuvenate the town centre in the second half of the 20th century, the section of road beyond the cross-roads has changed beyond all recognition. An equivalent view today would show the pedestrianised Crown Square precinct facing us across Commercial Way, with Crown House to the right and BHS to the left. Through traffic is diverted away from this part of the town. The buildings in the part of Chobham Road closer to the camera survived, however. Burton's building was put up in 1936; prior to that it was the site of the original Red House. At the time of writing, the premises are occupied by a motor spares and accessories dealer, and the building on the corner, which at the time of the photograph was the Red House Hotel, has now been painted bright blue and renamed O'Neill's!

Local DIY enthusiasts and people in the trade still think wistfully of Skeet & Jeffes - the place where you could wander around and come away with anything from half a dozen galvanised nails and an odd cup hook to a set of shelf brackets and a few wood screws - a facility sadly missed today, when nails, screws and the like come in little plastic packs, with far more in them than you need for the job! It was back in 1891 when Mr Skeet set up in business in Woking; he joined forces with Mr Jeffes ten years later, forming the partnership that was to last until the end of the 20th Century. Skeet & Jeffes moved to these premises in Chobham Road in 1908. Our photograph dates from 1953, and the intervening years have seen many changes. Most of the buildings on the right, including the Ritz Cinema, have disappeared. The massive 1970s Crown House office block today occupies much of the right hand side of Chobham Road, with the Visitor Information Centre on the corner of Commercial Road where Wearing's Chemist's shop once stood. Keen cyclists will remember Pearce's cycle shop, half way down on the left, once the meeting place of the Woking Cycling Club. BHS has now replaced most of these properties.

Above: More mature readers will almost certainly remember with affection Woking's long-serving public library when it was situated along Commercial Road. This rare photograph shows the building, and its origins as a former Wesleyan Chapel are obvious from this view of it. This was a busy spot, being on the corner of Commercial Road and Chapel Street, on the route of this number 34 bus from Guildford to Camberley, via Woking and Knaphill.

Libraries are the unsung heroes of our community, providing free access to a world of information, stimulation and inspiration long before the *Internet* was ever dreamed of! At the time of writing this popular position on Commercial Road is the home of two other organisations which could justly lay claim to the description 'unsung heroes'. Stirling work is done by Woking's Citizens Advice Bureau and the Association of Voluntary Services main offices.

Both pages: Home on leave for the weekend? This dashing young serviceman, caught on camera outside Woking Station, appears to be waiting for a taxi - or perhaps for his Mum? - to come and pick him up *(above)*. A few feminine hearts may have fluttered during his train journey; if the way to a man's heart is through his stomach, then surely the way to a woman's is by way of a smart uniform - and this handsome young man certainly fitted the bill! Our photograph bears no date, but the cars lined up along the kerbside (and by the 'No Waiting' sign) in the High Street are characteristic of three decades: the little 1960s Mini on the left; the Morris 1000, workhorse of the 1950s as well as the 60s, parked outside the Westminster Bank - and isn't that an old Ford Popular just behind it? Badge of the 1960s, the Mini was voted 'Car of the Century' in 1999, the year it celebrated its 40th birthday. An incredible 5.3 million Minis were sold, and Alec Issigonis was knighted for its innovative design. The Mini became the car to be seen in; Mary Quant, the Beatles, Peter Sellers, Spike Milligan - all had minis and loved them. Does this perhaps include the reader? The more mature driver, though, may recall driving a lovely old Ford Popular. Lovely in the abstract, perhaps? Remember how they would shudder when you went really fast - say

around 55 miles an hour? And the lack of heating? And the vacuum wipers that died when you put your foot down and flogged away like mad when you eased off the accelerator? A little knot of travellers has gathered outside the station entrance on the left; not the main entrance, as readers will already know, though certainly it is the one most widely used. People have often wondered why the station appears to have been built the wrong way round, but as the town developed to the north, calling for a more imposing north entrance, circumstances time and again prevented British Rail from purchasing the necessary land. The railway first came to Woking in 1838, when a line was built by the London and Southampton Railway between Nine Elms and Woking Common, quickly extended to Shapley Heath. Woking grew in importance after the Guildford to Portsmouth line opened, with goods trains, many of them bringing coal from the north, being re-routed here. As local landowners were persuaded to part with more land, the goods yards at Woking were extended to the north and south *(right)*. The wagons on the far right are standing in the York Road sidings, while to the left lie the Goldsworth sidings. The buildings of Woking town centre can be seen on the central horizon.

This page: Younger readers may have trouble pinpointing the spot where these buildings once stood *(above)*; today Premier House has replaced them. On the left are the offices of the Woking Water Company. The building on the right, near the junction of Percy Street and Commercial Road, has had a number of uses in its long history, but it was built as the Woking Public Halls, opening the door to the general public in 1896. It was a fine facility, having a 700 seat concert hall with a stage as well as a number of meeting rooms, which could be hired by organisations.

Many were the carol concerts, revues, church fetes and bring and buy sales held there, and in the days before Woking's cinemas opened, it was one of the first places to show films. It eventually became the Grand Theatre, and our more mature readers will remember the many happy evenings they spent enjoying the variety shows. The Grand was one of those wonderful, unsophisticated places of entertainment where an evening's programme might include a couple of singers, a comic duo, acrobats and musicians - some famous, others further down the bill, not so much so - and the public would go home satisfied at the end of the evening having enjoyed a varied and most enjoyable night out. During the 1920s 1/6d would buy you one of the 'popular' seats (the cheapest), while children could get in for 9d. The shows were so enjoyable that it was not unknown for youngsters to save their 3d-a-week pocket money for three whole weeks just so that they could go to the Grand Theatre again!

With the advent of the 'talkies', music hall went into decline, and when in 1935 the Woking UDC outgrew their Council Offices, they rented the first floor of the Grand Theatre to accommodate the Planning Department. The old Grand had several uses at the time of our second view *(left)*: Refuge Assurance, Prudential Assurance, and Newland Bros Coal and Coke Merchants all had their offices there.

Below: The Atalanta Ballroom was originally built as the Manse to the Wesleyan Chapel, which was on the opposite side of Commercial Road. The Wesleyan Chapel itself was later converted for use as Woking's library. The claims of many local men that they met their future wives at the 'Ata' are frequently disputed by the same women whose parents had forbidden them from going near the place. Few regular revellers would disagree that the ballroom had one of the best sprung dance floors in the south east, but it was not the quality of the woodwork that attracted squaddies from Inkerman Barracks at Knaphill every weekend. In later years many famous names performed at the Ata. Tom Jones and The Rolling Stones being the most memorable. It was a night to remember for Tom Jones when he performed here, for his first UK number one chart record topped the hit parade on the very same day. Plans to construct a 'much needed' car park on Commercial Road were first proposed in 1937. It was built soon afterwards. But it was not until the 1970s that the demolition men moved in to clear properties in the surrounding area. The 'new town centre' (as it was first known by local people) emerged from the rubble as houses and properties in this area were swept away. Soon afterwards the name *Wolsey Place* was adopted for the area.

Bottom: This view of High Street, Knaphill was recorded in the mid 1960s. The busy junction with The Broadway can be seen in the distance and a number of shoppers can be seen going about their business. The shops on the left of the picture include W.Rugleys, a popular draper and stationer, with W.E. Wheatlands further along the street. In the centre of the scene the large dark outline of Knaphill's Methodist Church can be seen. This well-supported place of worship was more modern than many churches in the district, being completed in the 1930s. On the right hand side of the photograph is the retail property which went on to be the home of Mann and Co., but which was originally built in 1913 as the local Co-op.

Retailing has seen many changes over the last half a century and most of the changes have had at least something to do with our love of the motorcar. In the days when most families relied on public transport to get around it was logical to position shops close to where we lived. Many of these, such as the Co-op, were part of larger organisations, but a considerable proportion were family-run concerns. The age of self-service supermarkets and the growth of car ownership resulted in the closure of scores of small grocers and retail businesses around Woking but happily most of the independent outlets of Knaphill have survived.

Changes were already afoot in Woking when this pigeon's eye view was captured in the town centre back in 1972. The Atalanta ballroom in the right foreground was already doomed, and within a few short months the demolition teams would move in on what had been a favourite venue during the swinging 60s. The next few years would see the rise and rise of The Peacocks Centre, the massive Toys R Us, The Wolsey Place Shopping Centre, and so much more that the people of Woking as yet could not visualise. The 1960s had already left their mark on the town:

Woking's excellent library can be seen in the left foreground, while in the background, dwarfed by the huge Premier House, we can pick out the Post Office, opened in April 1960. Premier House was only a decade or so old at the time of the photograph; constructed in the early 1960s by Norwich Union, the building was showing its age by the end of the 20th century. The year 2000 saw extensive modernisation carried out - plus a change of name to Globe House. Sharp eyed readers will spot the Co-op in the right background, with the fire station not too far away.

Left: A stark reminder of Woking's past history - Brookwood Hospital. Long gone now - and many would applaud the passing of the town's psychiatric hospital. The more sympathetic treatment in today's secure unit, built towards the left of this view in recent years, cannot be compared with the treatment of patients in the early years of the hospital. Surrey County Pauper Lunatic Asylum was known locally as simply Brookwood Asylum - and although today's more enlightened perception of mental illness and mental disability makes the name itself offensive to our ears, it was quite acceptable at the time. The 150 acres of land earmarked for the hospital cost Surrey County just £10,500 in 1860 (which sounds a snip at today's prices!), and Brookwood was opened in June 1867. Life was stark in the early days; patients were tucked away from the view of the outside world, and before central heating was installed, the luckless inmates were no strangers to hypothermia! Those who were able to work were the lucky ones; they were given employment around the hospital in the kitchens, the laundry, and on the asylum's own farm, which provided the establishment with vegetables and other fresh produce. Brookwood Hospital closed in 1981, and the area was subsequently redeveloped.

Below: A light sprinkling of snow adds a genuine touch of seasonal spirit to this charming view of Chertsey Road in 1964. Strings of fairy lights and stars emphasise the fact that Christmas has come around again - and Woking's coat of arms and motto, 'Fide et Diligentia (By Faith and Diligence), granted to the town in 1930, has been given pride of place. The magic of Christmas conjures images of sparkling trees, twinkling lights, parties, food and Santa Claus. Unfortunately it also means shopping, and these stores in Chertsey Road would have been very busy on the run up to the festive season. A clock in the distance informs us that it is 8.45pm, and perhaps today the street would still be crowded with late night shoppers. But maybe Christmas was already over? Undies displayed in the window on the left carry a sale notice. Were these bras really being sold for only 3/11d? (Just under 20p in today's currency.) Even allowing for the runaway inflation of the last 40 years, this price was a real snip.

This panoramic view across the northern part of Woking town centre and out to Horsell in the summer of 1970 was to change tremendously before the century was out. A new dual carriageway, Victoria Way, would slash across just below the line of the canal, which can be identified by the row of trees on our photograph, and the peaceful tree-lined road which runs off the picture to the north with barely a car in sight would later carry the heavy weight of traffic thundering to and from the M3. The Wheatsheaf Recreation Ground is clearly visible in the top right hand corner. There was a cricket pitch on Horsell Common, opposite the Wheatsheaf inn, certainly as early as 1870; a nine-acre area was laid out for public use in 1893, and further work was carried out here between the wars. Victoria Cottage Hospital can be seen on this picture, set back from Chobham Road with cars parked in front of it. This hospital was opened in September 1899 to commemorate the Diamond Jubilee of Queen Victoria. The building cost £4,200, and it initially had just seven beds; however, Woking was just beginning to attract industry around that time, with a corresponding rise in the population, and before long seven beds were no longer enough. Finally, opposite the Victoria Hospital we can pick out the Westgate Centre, destined for demolition as the new millennium dawns but enjoying rather more tranquil surroundings in this scene.

Bottom: How many readers still remember their co-op 'divi' number? Repeated time after time in those 'good old days' of shopping, those numbers are still there after all these years, filed away in some hidden pigeon hole in our brains! The Woking & District Co-operative Society built this branch on the corner of Percy Street and Church Street in the mid 1930s in the popular architectural style of the day. More mature readers may recall the old system of wires, cylinders and overhead tracks in the grocery department - and even the machine's little 'ping!' as it catapulted your cash away and delivered your change back at breakneck speed. All gone now, of course, and the site is today occupied by the offices of CAP Gemini. In 1955 the Woking Co-operative Society recorded sales worth £9,397,300, and a return in dividends on customers' purchases of £392,410.

The Co-operative movement started more than a century ago in Rochdale, Lancashire, where a group of local weavers paid £1 each to buy goods and open a shop. Customers were awarded a dividend on everything they bought. During the dark days of depression in the early 1920s and 30s the Co-op movement was responsible for a vast improvement in the standard of living of the average British working class person.

Right: An 'inconvenience' at the junction of Chertsey Road on the right and Commercial Road on the left, which would have left unsuspecting men searching their memories for

another loo. The ladies were OK - their facilities were off to the left of the picture! This was the early 1960s, and before long sweeping redevelopment would overtake the area. Even before the second world war the Council had been considering plans to redevelop the town centre - and then shelved for the duration. Plans were approved in 1960 to install a one way system, and demolition of various properties began in the late 60s. The junction of Chertsey Road and Commercial Road would in the course of time no longer exist; Commercial Road was later built across at this point, blocking it off to traffic.

How many of our readers remember Sallabank's, facing us on the corner of Walton Road? Sallabank's was a tobacconist as well as a barber, so you could have a short back and sides then pick up a packet of Players Weights and a box of Swan Vestas to take home with you.

people. Previously devastating diseases such as diphtheria, typhoid, scarlet fever and polio were eradicated. Vaccines were developed and became the most powerful weapons in the armoury of doctors fighting crippling diseases and premature deaths. Rising living standards, a better diet and, importantly, cleaner air would all enhance the health of the nation. Sadly the Victoria Hospital could not stand the test of time and was pulled down in the 1980s.

Top: Is this organised traffic chaos? Or simply traffic chaos? We are pretty sure, however, that in spite of indications to the contrary, the drivers involved in this near

Above: Queen Victoria's Diamond Jubilee was a good excuse for widespread joy and celebration throughout Britain and the Empire a little over a century ago in 1897. A little nearer home this lasting tribute to Britain's longest serving monarch was constructed, bearing her name. Situated alongside Chobham Road and Victoria Way, Victoria Hospital was a faithful servant to the citizens of Woking for over 80 years. The original building was extended in the 1920s and modifications to various aspects took place throughout its life. It is sobering to reflect on the fact that the hospital first saw service some 50 years before the National Health Service was introduced. From 1948 onwards the brainchild of Aneurin Bevan resulted in considerable improvements to the health of local

snarl-up on the corner of Chobham Road and Commercial Road really do know where they are going. A lone cyclist appears to be the only thing actually moving in this view - and he will have to have his wits about him if he doesn't want to end up looking at the flowers from the wrong end! Cycle helmets still lay many years in the future when a photographer captured this view on camera. Gammons - large in the background of the shot - had long been a favourite store with the ladies of Woking, and this was sale time. The people of Woking loved a bargain as much as the next person, and whether they were looking for curtaining, bedding, fashions or handbags, they were likely to find it at Gammons, and if it was reduced in price, then so much the better!

A huge board on the gable end of Tylers wine merchants informs passers by that they had 'branches from London to the Coast' - not that there were many passers by on the day this view of Chertsey Road was captured. Both above and on the window, smokers were advised that 'Players please' - and the well known brand of cigarettes have been pleasing smokers since their enduring slogan appeared back in the 1920s. Remember the rather romantic Players Navy Cut sailor on their early adverts? With

'Invincible' on his cap and a destroyer in the background, he smokes a contented pipe while reading his letter from home. It was 1971 before cigarette advertising and packets were required to carry a government health warning on the dangers of smoking. Tylers would eventually become Victoria Wines. Next door was the Albion Hotel, the second of that name on the same spot, the first Albion having been demolished in 1899. This well known watering hole would itself disappear as 1960s redevelopment swept the town.

This long-lens shot was taken looking almost due east across the town centre. Christ Church, just bottom left of centre, helps us situate ourselves, with Church Street running up vertically to the left and Commercial Road cutting up diagonally from the right. A number of interesting features of bygone Woking can be picked out, including the popular Atalanta dance hall and two of the town's old cinemas. The Atalanta is the white building on Commercial Road, below the large car park. Demolished in 1972, it stood on the corner of Bath Road, which is scarcely distinguishable from this angle. Away from the camera and to the left, the Ritz cinema is clearly visible on the top left hand corner of the junction of Chobham Road and Church Street. This cinema was opened in 1938; it eventually became part of the ABC chain, and survived longer than Woking's other picture houses. If we follow the railway line up from the station to the junction of Maybury Road and Duke Street, the greyish area shows the location of the Odeon, which closed in 1975. The Odeon was previously known as the Astoria. In its day, the Astoria was regarded as the ultimate in cinema luxury. It was built by a company called the London & Southern Super Cinemas Ltd, replacing the old Palace. The Palace Theatre was originally established as a variety and music hall at the end of the 19th century.

The vehicles in this view of Chertsey Road indicate the 1960s, a decade which saw the introduction of Woking's one way system. How many readers remember this parade of low shops on the right, and Burtons in the distance? Ladies may well remember shopping for their dresses, skirts and blouses at Elsie's, on the corner of Chertsey Road and Duke Street. Note the well known Hovis sign in the background; lovers of trivia will enjoy being reminded that the name Hovis (the winner of a competition to decide on a name for the bread) is a contraction of the Latin 'hominus vis' - 'the strength of man'. Hovis flour was first produced as long ago as 1885. Recent years have given us the Big Apple - a popular night spot among the young - in place of this row of shops.

Crown House is seen here under construction in 1977. Woking is part-way through its transformation process. Further back and to the left of the skeleton of Crown House, the Victoria Way car park can be seen, but there is as yet no sign of the big British Home Stores which later sprang up in the foreground of our picture, between Christ Church and Crown House. To the right, Dukes Court in particular is conspicuous by its absence. Facing Crown House across Chertsey Road we can see the Red House public house - later renamed the Firkin & Fahrenheit - while further back, keen-eyed readers will be able to pick out the houses on Stanley Road, home of pop icon Paul Weller.

Moving to the left, across Walton Road and towards the top left hand corner of the photograph, the Gas Works are plainly visible. The Gas Works were established in the early 1890s; the one-and-a-half acre site in Boundary Road was acquired for £649.10s.7d. by the newly-formed Woking District Gas Company. Prior to that, it had been commonland, and had it not been purchased by the Gas Company it was to have been used for housing. However, its proximity to the canal made it ideal for the gas works. A 60' high gasometer was built, the works opened in 1892, and the enterprise proved so successful that within less than a decade two extensions had been carried out to increase production.

At leisure

Under the watchful eye of their teacher (who seems a little over-dressed for the occasion), these young members of Woking Swimming Club launch out into the deep and learn how to swim. Though the lesson is obviously by instruction rather than example, we can understand the instructor's reluctance to get his kit off if he had to conduct several classes a day....
The weather looks reasonably pleasant in this view, but all the same there are still more people hanging around the pool than swimming in it. During the summer months, a sunny day spent at Woking Lido was a very popular way to pass the time. The weather had to be very warm before the crowds would brave a rash of goose pimples, though there were always a few intrepid souls who would defy the British weather and eagerly don their swimming costumes. Swimwear has changed a little since the date of this photograph; swimming caps, made of white rubber and with an uncomfortable strap that fastened under the chin, were customary among the girls, as we can see. Today, their use seems to have all but been abandoned - probably because they never did keep out the water anyway!
This swimming pool was built in the 1930s on the site of the original open air pool which had been built in Woking Park in 1910. The present modern indoor pool was to eventually replace this one.

Left: The event being celebrated here was important enough to call for a band; was it perhaps the launching of the cinema's new restaurant? Couples could now spend a pleasant evening at the ABC cinema, then end that special date with a memorable meal and a glass of wine. What they could not do, however, was cuddle together in double seats in the back rows! A petition to the management in 1960 drew the response that such seats had been declared illegal.

'Julia Misbehaves', released in 1948, was being screened at the time of the photograph. The ever popular Greer Garson starred in the film. Well known for her Anglo Irish charm, the flame-haired beauty began her career, as many film stars did, on the stage, making her stage debut in London in 1934. Garson herself loved to foster her Irish background and led the public to believe that she was born in County Down; it must have been the actress in her that promoted this little romantic fiction, because she actually came from Essex. It was her skilful performance as Mrs Chipping in 'Goodbye Mr Chips' that launched her in the direction of Hollywood, where she reigned as a star for many years.

Above: A fine sight after nightfall: the ABC Ritz ablaze with light. The cinema has long gone, of course, being replaced by a modern office block called Hollywood House, recalling the site's former association with the silver screen. Tony Hancock was starring in 'The Rebel' at the time of the photo-graph; how many readers were among the audience? Saturday morning cinema stirs even more memories, however. Remember the ABC Minors? And that catchy little song they sang? Readers who belonged to the children's club could more than likely still sing it if pushed, though they would probably rather not.... How many of those little ABC Minors badges still survive? Those were magic times; the vivid imagination of childhood coupled with innocent excitement and fun. There were no computer games back then; it was Roy Rogers and his four-legged friend Trigger; the black-masked Lone Ranger; Abbot and Costello; Old Mother Riley; often accompanied by shouts and cheers. Those were the days! The Ritz was built in 1937, the last of Woking's three old cinemas to open. It was the last, too, to close its doors when competition from television hit cinema audiences.

Bottom: Woking's first swimming pool was opened in Woking Park in 1910. Originally the water for the pool was pumped directly from the nearby Hoe Stream into the pool. It was not unheard of for the iron-stained water to leave a distinctive orange ring around the middle of unsuspecting bathers! The pool was revamped and rebuilt in the 1930s with fountains and play areas as depicted in this photograph. A new indoor swimming pool was built for Woking in the 1970s. Less than 20 years later the developers decided that the new facility was in the way of their aspirations for further changes and yet another pool was built on the site of the Lido in the park. Consequently, the Lido was closed and what we now know as 'The Pool in the Park' was built on the site. Later, the 'Leisure Lagoon' was added to the indoor pool. The trees seen running across the middle of the picture mark where the Hoe Stream runs and the field beyond became the site for the construction of the Leisure Centre in the 1970s.

Right: Question: What was pale pink, deafeningly noisy, and had one of the best sprung dance floors in the South East? No need to phone a friend - it was the old Atalanta Ballroom. The 'Ata' might have been a bit on the rowdy side, but it was the place to go if you wanted good live music, from R & B to the Twist, from visiting performers or from Bob Potter's resident band. August 19th 1963 saw the walls of the building shake to the sound of the Rolling Stones - a gig which stands out in the memories of those lucky enough to have been there that night. The Atalanta is automatically linked with bands, discos, noise - and on occasions, even fights. But the Ata was more than just a night spot, as daytime fixtures also featured on the programme of events. Perhaps you were one of the terrified 10 year olds in the audience when 'Dr Who and the Daleks' came to exterminate the town? You will remember that wishing for a Tardis to carry you off to another time zone did absolutely no good at all! The demolition squad were already at work on the building when our photo was taken in 1972. The site would soon be redeveloped, and the old Atalanta would be merely a memory.

A family snapshot from 1965 captured this scene along Ryden's Way, Old Woking. At the time of writing this stretch of road looks remarkably similar - and people still park their cars on the grass which forms the central reservation. Originally, Ryden's Way was intended to form part of Woking's southern bypass. The Ford van brings back nostalgic memories. It would have been a familiar sight on Britain's roads in the 1960s, and was in direct competition to the Morris Minor van which was slightly more numerous. The reliable work-horse of plumbers, builders, butchers and bakers later found worthwhile use as the cheap and cheerful family motor. The mid 1960s saw the growth of privately-owned motorcars as motoring became a realistic aspiration for anyone with a steady job.

As all our older readers will remember, Empire Day was once a huge date in the school year. There was a suitable buildup, of course, to the big day - 24th May - when children were taught the importance of the British Empire. They learned how fortunate they were to live in the British Isles and to be part of a vast Empire 'upon which the sun never set'. Most of all they acquired a pride in their British citizenship and a fierce allegiance to the British flag. Empire Day was looked forward to eagerly weeks in advance, and when the day dawned, children from every school formed a long procession and marched proudly behind their flags. Huge crowds turned out to watch the parade, everyone in their Sunday best, parents' necks craned to catch sight of their own children as they marched through the town. Year after year the procession took the same route, which took them along Commercial Road and out to Woking Park. Then it was fun and games time, with races and sports. Maybury School children were marching by as a photographer snapped them in 1906. This was just two years after Empire Day was officially recognised, and the 24th May - the anniversary of Queen Victoria's birthday - designated as a day of promotion in schools of 'training for Empire citizenship'.

Events & occasions

Left: number of school flags are visible in our second photograph, dating from 1913: Church Street School, Woking Village; Goldsworth Council School, and Maybury School. A company of boy scouts (and a few uniformed girls) form an important part of the parade. The scouting movement was formed in 1908, following the publication of Sir Robert Baden-Powell's book 'Scouting for Boys'. The book had been intended for use by existing youth organisations, but it proved to be the beginning of a new one. Baden-Powell's ideas on the training of young boys differed from others, as he included such activities as signalling, rope-knotting, mapping, first aid and other skills needed in camping and similar outdoor activities which developed self-reliance. The movement became popular and quickly spread from Britain to other countries - and a similar movement was set up, of course, for girls.

Across the crowd, babies and toddlers are being held up by mums and dads so that they could get a better view of their older brothers and sisters who were so proud to march for their country. The following year, 1914, would see the cream of Britain's young men march off to fight for King and country in the Great War. But that's another story....

Above: 'We fought for humanity - and won!' reads the huge banner hung across the front of the Grand Theatre, while 'God save the King' and 'Long may peace continue' decorated Woking's council offices. This was 1919, and Woking had turned out in force for the peace celebrations. The Great War had been a long one, and many were the horror stories told of the mud, the blood, and the great human suffering and loss. At last the end had come; in a railway carriage in France Germany surrendered to the Allies, the Kaiser abdicated and fled into exile in Holland, and in the year 1918 the four-year war officially came to an end at the 11th hour of the 11th day of the 11th month. An appalling total of 8.5 million people were killed in the Great War; in Woking, 550 local people had lost their lives. It was appropriate to have a suitable memorial designed and the design of Mr Doyle Jones was chosen. At a cost of £2,000 the new memorial was produced and placed in Sparrow Park; the new cenotaph was unveiled on 24th May 1922 - Empire Day - by Field Marshall Sir William Robertson.

Right: Here is a view which raises more questions than it answers. A large crowd of men, women and children of all ages has gathered outside the new Wesleyan church, which is still in the process of construction; obviously something important is taking place, yet there appears to be no real focus to the crowd's attention. This busy and utterly fascinating photograph gives us the opportunity to travel back through the years and glimpse Commercial Road - and some of the people of Woking - as they were in 1904. What strikes us right away is the elegance of the ladies, with their beautiful lace collars, nipped in waists, parasols, and skirts that swept the ground, and the panache of the young men (who said posers were a 21st Century phenomenon?) with their straw boaters and air of masculinity. But think how those corsets would have dug in and restricted your breathing, and how, in an era that pre-dated the washing machine, those long sweeping skirts would have swept up the mud!
Signs in the background advertise 'the novelty of the moment' in millinery, blouses, costumes, and a great deal more, at Archibolds, and inform passers by that this was 'the site for the new Wesleyan church and school'. The building appears to be almost complete, though scaffolding and long ladders remain; note the man at work high above the crowd.

What was this event which called Woking's Muslims out in force? A festival? The visit of a special speaker? A wedding? Unfortunately, this fascinating photograph carried neither a date nor any details; all we can say with any certainty is that a good time was obviously being enjoyed by all, as people leave the marquee and gather in groups to meet and chat. Our readers, however, could well remember the occasion and be able to shed more light on the mystery. As far back as the late 19th Century, Woking's Muslim community - most of them students at the Oriental Institute - were in the fortunate position of being able to worship in their own mosque. Dr Gottlieb Leitner, Professor in Arabic and Mohammedan Law, founded the Institute in the 1880s as a centre for linguistics and eastern culture, and had the Shah Jehan Mosque built in 1889 to serve the spiritual needs of the students. The mosque, which remains one of Woking's most remarkable buildings, was the very first to be built in the UK - and cost its architects, who were unused to undertaking such exotic contracts, more than a few headaches during its construction. During the first world war the government built a Muslim cemetery on Horsell Common for the burial of Indian soldiers killed whilst serving in Europe.

mess and misery caused by the 1968 floods over 30 years ago. The stinking water ruined carpets and caused interior woodwork such as skirting boards and door frames to warp and come away from the brick and stonework. Plaster came away from walls and it was weeks before life returned to anything like normal.

Top: Proud men of the Woking Electric Supply Company parade for the Home Guard along Walton Road. They were part of the national force numbering around one million men, formerly known as the Local Defence Volunteers and initially armed with a variety of garden tools, makeshift spears and the odd gamekeeper's shotgun. As the war progressed uniforms and weapons became more freely available to the Home Guard whose membership ranged from enthusiastic lads in their late teens to seasoned veterans of the Great War and even earlier conflicts. Men working in reserved occupations were the backbone of many Home Guard platoons as far as a potential fighting force was concerned. The Nazis attempted to demoralise and discourage volunteers with broadcasts suggesting that they would be shot as members of 'murder bands' and 'cowardly snipers' once the invasion got underway. Thankfully it never did.

Above: The High Street, Old Woking, as it appeared in November 1968. Flooding had made the road impassable and brought misery to scores of householders who occupied properties lining this normally busy road. The Crown and Anchor public house was one of the first buildings to succumb to the rising water. The petrol station (which sold E.P petrol at the time) followed soon afterwards along with the retail shop property belonging to Old Woking Service Station. Flooding was to return to Old Woking at the beginning of the new Millennium. The water's return in November 2000 compelled residents and businesses to lay out sandbags in their doorways and take as many precious belongings as possible upstairs to relative safety. People in Old Woking still remember the

As we look from the darker interior of the building towards a sunlit Duke Street, the brightness has almost reduced the young builder on the right to a cut out figure, silhouetted against the light. A second, hard to spot, man is working on the left of the view. Surrounded by piles of rubble, ripped-up floorboards and discarded old doors - the normal kind of debris that was all part of a normal day's work - the men were hard at work on the reconstruction of the Astoria Cinema. This same site had offered different kinds of entertainment in the town for many years. From

899 the Palace Theatre had stood there; built as a
music hall and variety theatre, the Palace had
installed projection equipment as moving pictures
gained in popularity. Its owner, Frederick Iverson,
sold the facility in 1925 and it was rebuilt as the
Astoria. Now, a second change was in progress; like

a Phoenix from the ashes, the new Odeon would
before long rise from these heaps of rubble. Part of
the Rank organisation, the Odeon served Woking's
cinemagoers well for many years before it fell victim
to declining audiences. It showed its last film and
closed its doors for good in April 1975.

Both pages: In 1939 Britain's Prime Minister Neville Chamberlain had made his announcement to the waiting people of Britain that '...this country is at war with Germany.' The country rolled up its sleeves and prepared for the inevitable. This war would be different from other wars. This time planes had the ability to fly further and carry a heavier load, and air raids were fully expected. Air raid shelters were obviously going to be needed, and shelters were built on open places across towns and cities.

By the time war was declared an army of volunteers of both sexes had already been recruited to form an Air Raid Protection service. At first ARP personnel were unpaid volun-

teers but when war broke out in September 1939 they became paid staff. It was their job to patrol specified areas, making sure that no chinks of light broke the blackout restrictions, checking the safety of local residents, being alert for gas attacks, air raids and unexploded bombs. The exceptional work done by Air Raid Wardens in dealing with incendiaries, giving first aid to the injured, helping to rescue victims from their bombed-out properties, clearing away rubble, and a thousand and one other tasks became legendary; during the second world war nearly as many private citizens were killed as troops - and many of them were the gallant ARP wardens. At the beginning of the war Sir Anthony Eden, Secretary of State for War, appealed in a radio broadcast for men between

7 and 65 to make up a new force, the Local Defence Volunteers, to guard vulnerable points from possible Nazi attack. Within a very short time the first men were putting their names down. At first the new force had to improvise; there were no weapons to spare and men had to rely on sticks, shotguns handed in by local people, and on sheer determination. Weapons and uniforms did not become available for several months.

In July the Local Defence Volunteers was renamed the Home Guard, and by the following year were a force to be reckoned with. Television programmes such as 'Dad's Army' have unfortunately associated the Home Guard with comedy, but in fact they performed much important work. The Guard posted sentries to watch for possible aircraft or parachute landings at likely spots such as disused aerodromes, golf courses on the outskirts of towns, local parks and racecourses.

They manned anti-aircraft rocket guns, liaised with other units and with regular troops, set up communications and organised balloon barrages.

Other preparations were hastily made. Place names and other identifying marks were obliterated to confuse the enemy about exactly where they were. Notices went up everywhere giving good advice to citizens on a number of issues. 'Keep Mum - she's not so dumb' warned people to take care what kind of information they passed on, as the person they were speaking to could be an enemy.

Older readers will remember how difficult it was to find certain items in the shops during the war; combs, soap, cosmetics, hairgrips, elastic, buttons, zips - all were virtually impossible to buy as factories that once produced these items had been turned over to war work. Stockings were in

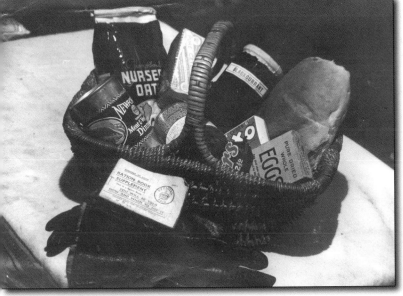

short supply, and resourceful women resorted to colouring their legs with gravy browning or with a mixture of sand and water. Beetroot juice was found to be a good substitute for lipstick. Clothes rationing was introduced in 1941, and everyone had 66 coupons per year. Eleven coupons would buy a dress, and sixteen were needed for a coat. The number of coupons was later reduced to 40 per person. People were required to save material where they could - ladies' hemlines went up considerably, and skirts were not allowed to have lots of pleats. Some found clever ways around the regulations by using materials that were not rationed. Blackout material could be embroidered and made into blouses or skirts, and dyed sugar sacks were turned into curtains.

'V' for Victory - the message on the banner couldn't be plainer! The celebration, of course, was VE Day in 1945, and now the war was over it was party time in Cherry Street, Goldsworth. The children had seen few treats during their short lives, and doing the best they could with the ingredients they could get hold of, these mothers managed to conjure up sandwiches, cake, buns and even jelly to give the all the kiddies in the street the best party they'd ever had. Food was still strictly rationed - including sweets - and these children had grown up

on a basic diet that held few luxuries. Clothing, too, was on ration, and people had to 'make do and mend' whenever they could; by the end of the war most women's wardrobes were looking decidedly tired. Everyone was looking forward to the future years, and especially to the end of rationing - which did not fully come about until 3rd July 1954. Cherry Street was a small cul-de-sac off Poole Road, and a train on the railway embankment can just be seen above the victory banner. The houses were demolished in the early 1970s to make way for an industrial estate.

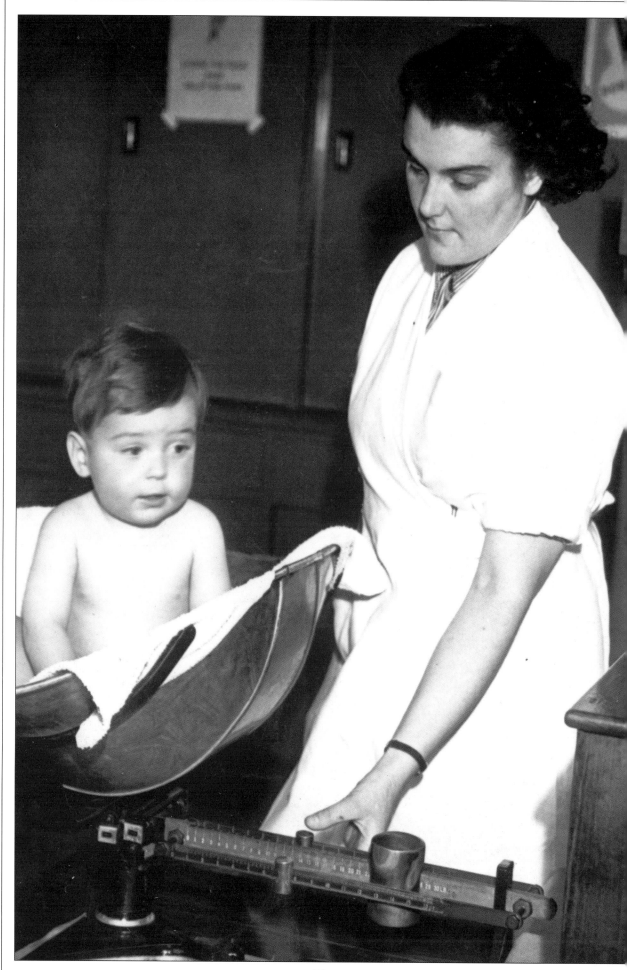

Both pages: It was possibly the acute wartime shortages of food and supplies which made doctors, health workers and mothers alike very aware of the health of the new generation, and children were carefully weighed, measured and immunised against the illnesses that had at one time meant disfigurement or even death *(facing page)*. A vaccine for polio, the scourge of former years which left behind its terrible mark of wasted and useless limbs, only came later, however. American scientist Jonas Edward Salk developed a vaccine in 1955, and an oral vaccine was produced in 1960. The vaccines brought the dreaded disease under control and today polio is rarely seen. On a day to day basis, vitamins were vital to the health of children, and long before the advent of the cod liver oil capsule, the recommended spoonful of cod liver oil was administered to the youngest children every day in schools and nurseries around the country during the 1940s. Children might have screwed up their noses at the fishy taste, but the nourishing cod liver oil went a long way towards keeping them healthy. The vitamin-packed orange juice was far more palatable, and artful mothers would often use the orange juice as a bribe: no cod liver oil, no orange juice. Following hard on the heels of the oil, the juice took away the distinctive taste that was disliked by so many children. Ante-natal clinics

did all they could to check on the diet, blood pressure and vitamin intake of mothers to be; our carefully posed photograph, taken in an ante-natal clinic in the 1930s, records at least the cleanliness and tidiness that was to their great credit *(bottom)*. And when the tiny new citizen finally arrived, there were health visitors to pay friendly calls on families in their homes to check on the health and happiness of mothers and babies *(left)*. National Dried Milk for babies was also made available to mothers, and before today's push towards natural feeding NDM was for decades very much in vogue. We need to remember that at the time of these photographs the National Health service did not exist, and in fact the NHS only came into operation after World War II in July 1948.

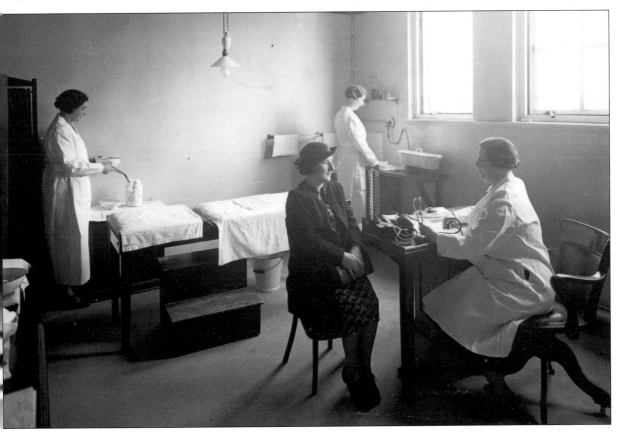

On the move

Unlike many parts of the town, Woking Station is still recognisable almost 50 years on! With just a couple of vehicles, two cycles leaning against the wall and a traveller or two in the shot, the station was remarkably quiet when this view was captured back in 1953. The news vendor who waited patiently by the entrance for customers was far from being the first of his kind; Woking Station's newspaper seller was mentioned in H G Wells' science fiction novel 'The War of the Worlds' back in 1896! Advertisements and timetables relieved the outside wall, and though travellers were unable to refresh themselves with the Guinness which was so prominently advertised, W H Smith's kiosk would at least have been able to provide them with a tube of sweets for their journey. The British public have believed that Guinness was good for them since the drink was first advertised in 1929, and many clever slogans have been produced over the years: 'Tall, Dark and Have Some', 'Seven Million Every Day and Still Going Down' and notably 'I've Never Tried it Because I Don't Like it'. And remember 'Guinness is Good for you - Just think what Toucan do'?

eft: Eight twenty-eight in the morning, and Platform at Woking Station is still crowded with office orkers, though a few ladies on the right have possibly ecided to take advantage of the warm weather and ake a shopping trip. We note that most of these aiting passengers are men carrying briefcases and ressed in business suits and ties, on their way to the ffice; only one 'city gent' is wearing a bowler, once the adge of the smart business man. The above the knee emline worn by one of the few young ladies present lentifies this as the 1960s, when 'office girls' still lade tea for the men, whose posteriors were firmly ositioned on the seats of leadership and management. ut the worm was about to turn, and in a male ominated society women were soon daring to demand qual rights and opportunities. Woking Station had by le 1960s grown to be the busiest in the county, largely le to electrification. The conversion of the lines had egun in the 1920s, and in 1937 it was Woking's turn. long with electrification came the total rebuilding of le station to the red brick and cream tiled, typically 930s, building we still have today.

Below: It was a quiet, sunny day in The Broadway when a photographer decided to record this view. A number of people were taking advantage of the warm sunshine to get out and about, and some were already aboard the Aldershot & District bus to Guildford through Sutton Green, the Number 29 route. Today, this is a scene to stir memories as we look back to the way things were before Alldays supermarket replaced Barclays Bank. But if things had gone the way of popular demand, this area would have developed rather differently. The entrance to the railway station, just off picture to the right, had long been a disappointment to local people, who thought that Woking Station deserved a more worthy entrance. As far back as the 1880s this had been a factor to consider, and when the railway was widened and the station was rebuilt, the London and South Western Railway approached the Rural Highway Board with a view to acquiring more land. They were turned down. A second chance came in 1897 when the original Albion Hotel was demolished; there was a call for a more imposing station entrance and a civic square to be laid out. Sadly, the proposal was rejected, and Woking Station kept its unimpressive entrance.

Allo, allo, allo - what's going on here? Not exactly chaos; let's call it moderate confusion. The drivers making their way from The Broadway and along the High Street seem to be getting things right, but an air of bewilderment surrounds the little knot of pedestrians crossing the road. However, the long arm of the law in the shape of a friendly PC is here to sort it all out. This was May 1969, and major changes were in progress in the town centre. Only

few days before, Woking's one way system had un in the opposite direction along this stretch of oad. The motorists themselves were beginning to esign themselves to this kind of thing; after all, vhat was new about it? It had all happened before - this was just the latest in a series of similar frustrating changes, and the 'Alice through the Looking Glass' approach to motoring (head off in the opposite direction to your destination) was becoming familiar to drivers around Woking.

At the shops

This wonderfully nostalgic scene was captured in Chertsey Road on VJ Day. Towns and cities all over the country put out the flags and prepared to celebrate as soon as they heard the news of the Japanese surrender on 14th August, 1945. This finally marked the end of all hostilities, although the formalities were not completed until September 2nd, 1945. The anniversary of the Victory in Japan is now commemorated as VJ Day, and the unconditional surrender of Germany on 7th May is remembered as VE Day - Victory in Europe. As far as most people were concerned, once we had defeated Hitler the war was as good as won, and VE parties and celebrations were held in May - but that didn't stop anyone from partying again in August. Britain did not return to normal overnight, however. Rationing remained in force for many years. Boots and its neighbours will have no luxury items to offer, and the jaunty shoppers who are looking in the shop windows will still have to make do with the meagre range of wartime supplies. The elegant timbered building a few doors along from Boots is the old Post Office; on the corner is Barclays Bank, and we have a clear view of the railway station directly ahead of us.

There is no hint of the changes to come in this view of Chertsey Road as it was back in 1957. The heart of Woking's shopping centre, Chertsey Road was a place of small shops and well known names, both local and national. Remember trying on shoes in Freeman, Hardy and Willis? There was a time when high streets around the country were sprinkled with an assortment of different shoe shops: Freeman, Hardy and Willis, Saxone, Dolcis, Timpson, Stead and Simpson, Barratts, Bata - there they all were. Is it imagination, or are there fewer shoe shops about today? Next door, of course, was Timothy Whites (which would before long add 'and Taylor' to their name), with the good old Home & Colonial stores adjoining. The rain has not deterred a few shoppers from turning out, and a number of them were on bikes. A basket attached to the handlebars has to have been one of the cycle manufacturer's key inventions! A young mother struggles around the shops with a young baby in a pram and a second child in tow; slightly easier to cope with in today's pedestrianised shopping centres - at least she would not have to dodge the traffic!

If you want to know the time, ask a policeman. So the old maxim advises us, though this gentleman chatting with a member of the local constabulary on Burton's corner could just as easily be asking the way, or simply passing the time. Whatever town or city you visited Burton's was impossible to miss, and the Woking branch, on the corner of Chertsey Road and Chobham Road, was built in 1936 in the unmistakable Burton's style. As was the norm, the names of other branches were framed above each window; we can make out Blackpool and Chester above and behind the two men. Montague Burton's good quality menswear has been a firm favourite with gentlemen for many years. The story goes that when soldiers were demobbed after military service they were given vouchers to be outfitted at Burtons. They went along to the nearest branch and were kitted out in what was termed 'the full Monty' - a phrase which has in recent years come to mean something quite the opposite of a full suit of clothes!

The Burton's building was constructed in the garden of the original Red House Hotel, and its successor, also the Red House (later the Firkin & Fahrenheit and now O'Neill's), can be seen to the left of Burtons. The 1905 Guide to Woking assures us that it had good stabling as well as a billiards room.

Left: Robertson Brothers, a household name in household furnishings, traded from several units in Chertsey Road. This was the place to go whether you were looking for a new three piece suite, a dining table and chairs, a nest of tables, or you simply wanted to browse around the well stocked showrooms to gather a few ideas for your ideal home. Robertsons ran an across the board service. They would not only help you find that new home through their estate agency, but would come along with their removals van and move you in - and if you had the wherewithal they would also fill your home with new furnishings. This view was recorded in January 1954; ten years on, Robertsons was gone, along with the adjoining greengrocer's shop, to be replaced by Tesco's super-market. Interestingly, Tesco's founder Sir John Cohen was famous for his golden rule, 'Pile it high, sell it cheap' - a rule which was to be the making of Sir John's fortune. But nothing ever stays the same, and today Tesco's has been replaced by The Rat & Parrot.

Above: Bicycles dominate this 1950s view of High Street. Several machines can be seen casually propped up at the side of the pavement while owners go about their business unseen. Having your bike stolen was less of a worry at this time, and cyclists would have laughed out loud at the idea of having to remove their saddle to deter thieves. It was clearly a pleasant day when the photographer recorded the scene judging by the summer dresses and extended canvass canopies along the street. The weighty sunshades were there to protect produce and customers from the effects of the sun. The third one of these blinds away from the camera denotes the position of the Woking branch of J.Sainsburys. Similar retail chains had sprung up from the middle of the 1800s onwards, thanks largely to the growth of the railways and availability of all kinds of pre-packed products. Brand names such as Cadbury, Rowntrees, Lipton and Hornimans accompanied the phenomenon, adding to the number of products which could be found in this and other branches of Sainsbury's and similar stores in the district. This was not the first branch of Sainsbury's to serve the people of Woking. The High Street store had opened in the 1930s, superseding an earlier branch on Chertsey Road. The railway station can just be seen at the top right of the photograph.

Below: This familiar view of Chertsey Road dates from about 1960. Virtually everyone in the photograph is female - drawn to this part of the town by the quality and variety of shops to be found. This, however, was a characteristic that could not be taken for granted and the Council was acutely aware of the need to keep pace with developments in retailing if Woking was to hold the attention of its shopping public. Despite this, there was a conflict between the interests of the town as a whole and the interests of some local businessmen, several of whom had seats on the Council.

It was not until late 1960 that serious retail development got underway, and not until 1968 that demolition in the 'central area' began. An eight-acre site would become Woking's new, partly-covered shopping area. It was fully pedestrianised, separating shoppers and motor traffic as recommended by reports written over a decade earlier. Many small independent shops would be lost in the changes which followed, but the other side of the coin was the influx of national high-street names, which for so long had been lacking.

Right: It's a fine sunny day; sun blinds have been let down to protect goods in the shop windows, and the owner of this neat little convertible Austin with a West Sussex registration number has thrown caution to the winds and let down his hood. We can't help but notice that he has rather cheekily parked right next to a sign which reads 'No waiting this side today'; he obviously regards the notice as a suggestion rather than an instruction! Goldsworth Road was very quiet at the time, with no sign of a police officer (had traffic wardens been introduced at the time of this undated photograph, we wonder?). But the driver who believed that his small misdemeanour had gone unnoticed little thought that a photographer was nearby to record the scene for posterity! Phillips Bargain Stores are advertising their men's clothing and footwear, but the displays in their windows show that their range of goods did not stop there. Today, along with many other changes, the rather smart Pizza Express has replaced Phillips', while the left side of Goldsworth Road is lined with modern red brick shops and office blocks.

This view was taken from the corner of Chapel Street and High Street. We are looking along High Street towards the corner with Chertsey Road, where at the time of our photograph the Albion Hotel would have stood. Next to the off-licence on the corner of Chapel Street we can see Colmans, the big furnishing store. R & S Colman was a long-established Woking business; an advertisement in a local guide book of 1905 informs us that in addition to supplying items such as 'furniture, carpets, lino, pianos, textiles, china, glass, clocks, tools, cycles, cutlery', they undertook 'Removals and warehousing' using 'improved methods' and 'up to date vans', and they also promised to send out 'Competent men ... at short notice to fix blinds, poles, carpets etc'. The business eventually became part of Courts' furnishing chain. Next to Colmans we can see Edwards' prominent shop sign. Edwards was a drapery business. In later years this shop closed, and the premises were converted into two separate shop units. The buildings along High Street were relatively unaffected by more recent major developments in the town centre, as it was the area to the north which was chosen as the focus for the modern shopping centres, pedestrian precincts and high-rise office blocks which were to become synonymous with late-20th century Woking.

Below: The early decades of the 20th century saw Chertsey Road established as Woking's principal shopping street, boasting a series of leading retail chains. By the early 1930s Chertsey Road had a Sainsbury's, a Boots, a MacFisheries, a Timothy Whites - and, of course, a Woolworths. Many of these retail giants began as family businesses which then prospered and spread into virtually every shopping area in the country, overshadowing the small local traders. So, for instance, Boots was started by Nottingham's Jesse Boot, and Woollies by the American brothers Woolworth. Woolworths, known in America as the '5 and 10 cent Stores', came to Britain with the tag of '3d and 6d Stores', and opened a branch in Chertsey Road in 1926. The original store did not have the extensive frontage seen in this photograph. The portion of the site at the end farthest from the camera used to be John Bright's tailors shop, one of the few properties in Woking which had the misfortune to be bombed during the second world war. In 1958 Woolworths expanded, pulling down their old premises and building the modern store pictured here. With its multiple doors and its modern glass-and-steel design, Woollies seemed like the ultimate shopping experience, and any readers who worked there, either full-time or as Saturday girls, will probably remember feeling very pleased with themselves for landing such a good job.

Bottom: Remember Sports House in Commercial Road? Little boys and big ones alike (not to mention the little girls!) spent a lot of their time gazing into the windows of this marvellous store. Sports House opened in the mid 1930s - hard times for some families - and though there were always the more affluent to patronise the establishment, for many youngsters the store remained a 'look but don't touch' shop. But there was nothing to stop them from dreaming of the time when they would be able to afford that beautiful willow cricket bat, that smooth leather football, or the pair of roller skates so temptingly displayed in the window. Here were toys and games galore: Dinky cars to collect; toy farms with a full complement of sheep, cows and horses; forts with armies of toy soldiers; train sets complete with track,

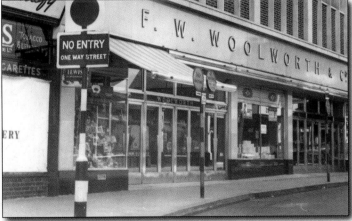

tunnels, bridges, stations, and miniature station masters, and Meccano sets, with which you could build your own fantastic machines. Here were fishing rods and keep nets, floats and feather flies. Plenty to keep a boy dreaming. But hope, they say, springs eternal - and the tide turns at low water as well as at high....

Making a living

Courageous men doing a valuable job: members of Woking's Fire Brigade pose alongside their vehicles as a photographer records the moment for posterity. It was built in 1928 and the builders of this rather attractive facility would surely have been dismayed if they had known that it would be replaced only 50 or so years on. Setting up Woking's first official fire service in 1895 was a rather hit and miss undertaking based on the 'yes we will no we won't' decisions of successive Councils, and as a result little cash was spared for the project. Sites were set up in Chertsey Road, Woking, Kiln Bridge, Old Woking and Knaphill. Sheds of corrugated iron, compared by the locals with bathing huts, were the unlovely homes of the £300-worth of new equipment; each site was allotted a 35ft ladder, two shorter ladders, and a jumping sheet. The onset of World War I in 1914 saw the equipment sadly out of date, and in 1919 a new Dennis motor engine was acquired. It was not before time - the old steam engine had coughed its last while pumping water out of the swimming pool. The fire station pictured here was built on the site of St Dunstan's Catholic Presbytery at a cost of £4,900, and the brigade moved in on 21st July 1928. It was replaced by the modern building we know today in 1981.

You had only to blink your eyes in the 1960s (or so it seemed), and another well-known building had disappeared. The Albion Hotel, which had not long before stood on this site, had been quenching Woking's thirst since the turn of the 20th Century. It was the second hotel of that name to occupy the same site; the original Albion had been built between 1856-1857 by Reuben Percy (who gave his name to Percy Street). The office block which we know today as Albion House would eventually emerge from this building site, photographed here from a dizzying height. Built by Norwich Union at the cost of £500,000, the new building provided the town with a number of shops and a pub for those who like a pint or three, as well as offices. You might be forgiven for supposing that the new pub would have been named The Albion, if only for old time's sake. But what did we get? The Boston Exchange. To the committee who chose it, the name obviously appeared logical. But who was it who once said that a camel is a horse designed by a committee?

the only way was up for the ambitious and inventive Morris, and in 1912 he opened a car factory near Oxford, producing the first Morris Oxford car in 1913. He can be said to have revolutionised the British car industry through his introduction of low price, mass produced cars.

Top: In January 1971, demolition of the old prison at Knaphill was underway. This fine edifice has a fascinating history. Standing in 63 acres of land and surrounded by an 18' high wall, the prison was described as 'one of the most impressive buildings in Woking'. Its clock tower was 190' high, and the prison was sited on one of the highest parts of Knaphill. When it was opened in 1859, it was the first

Above: Some guys have all the luck - and this unknown Woking mechanic was fortunate enough to get his head under the bonnet of a marvellous old Morris Eight. Can't you almost smell that leather upholstery?

The Eight was produced for the 1935 season - and the four door saloon very quickly established itself as a runaway success. At £142 it was more expensive than its similar rivals, but even so, drivers loved it; the Eight was in later years to earn a reputation as the car driven by district nurses before there were Morris Minors! During the 1930s it became the best seller of the decade, with 221,000 Morris Eights being produced. When William Richard Morris, 1st Viscount Nuffield, went into business as a cycle repairer back in 1892, he had no way of knowing that he would one day become known as Father of the British motor car industry, and that his name would become a household word. But from the cycle workshop

prison in the country designed especially for disabled prisoners. Inmates appear to have been well fed and looked after, at a cost to the state of £31.13s.0d per convict per year in 1866/7. At an inquest in 1869, held after the Governor had been stabbed with a nail by one of the prisoners, it was reported that the convicts were served 'steaks, chops, jellies, wines and other luxuries'. The Governor scarcely seems to have deserved the treatment he got, and not surprisingly, the jury formed the opinion that inmates were treated too well. In later investigations the reports of high living were proved to be totally without foundation. The building operated as a prison for less than four decades; in 1895 it became Inkerman Barracks, and was assigned to the 26th Company Royal Engineers. From 1947 to 1965 the barracks was the home of the Military Police. In 1965 the barracks were closed, and in 1971 the building was demolished.

This charming scene was captured along Woking's Maybury Road in the years soon after the last war. Character is added to the photograph by the Woking UDC tipper truck sitting high and proud on its hard springs, as if protecting the gang of workmen from the oncoming traffic. There seems to be little urgency and less drama at the roadworks. Somewhere, just out of sight, there is bound to be a well-used kettle, boiling water for refreshing tea on top of a tightly-stoked brazier. The relative tranquility of Maybury Road would be interrupted from time to time by the sound of railway engines on the

rack just a few yards above. Note how the ath of the track bed is delineated by the turdy wooden fence, running as straight as an rrow away from the centre of Woking. Much f the success enjoyed by the town in post-war ears came as a result of its good road and rail onnections. People were attracted to the area from London, which faced an uphill struggle to rebuild and rehouse her population after the devastation caused by the Blitz. Woking was relatively unscathed and the architects of the 'Greater London Plan' suggested that around 3,000 Londoners should relocate to the town in the years after the war.

Greenfield School - the learning years

N o one ever quite forgets their school days - possibly the best days of our lives even if we didn't recognise it at the time. How many readers, we wonder, have happy memories of Greenfield School?

The large impressive Edwardian house, which is now Greenfield, stands squarely on the corner of Brooklyn Road and the Guildford Road. Its exterior belies its true size, and once inside visitors not infrequently liken it to the Tardis of 'Dr Who' fame, since it is deceptively spacious and extensive.

The school can trace its origins back to 1922. In that year the large building known as Denham House at the foot of Constitution Hill became a Dame School, charging modest fees for the education of local boys and girls. By 1935 the school had been purchased by a Mr and Mrs Wilkinson, who changed its name to Greenfield School. Although most of the rooms were used as classrooms, lodgers apparently lived in the attic, and it was here that a serious fire broke out, leading to the death of one of the residents. Blackened roof beams exposed during the re-tiling of the roof in 1990 bore silent witness to the fire that had threatened the entire building.

Some time between the Wilkinson's purchase and 1948, Henry Dafter Quartermaine, local entrepreneur and property owner bought the house, leasing it back to the Wilkinsons who continued to run the school. Henry Quartermaine had three times held office as Chairman of Woking Council, and as a well known local businessman was reputed to 'own half the town' Many of his properties would eventually become part of Greenfield's inheritance.

Henry Quartermaine died in 1941; seven years later Mr and Mrs Wilkinson decided to give up the proprietorship of Greenfield, which was offered to two of Quartermaine's relatives, Ruth Hicks and Joyce Pearce, through the trustees of the Quartermaine estate. The timing was opportune, since both women had reached a point in their lives that facilitated change.

Ruth Hicks had lived as a child in Weston Super Mare, and came to Surrey as a maths teacher, eventually achieving deputy headship of Woking Girls' Grammar School.

Below: *Henry Dafter Quartermaine, property owner and benefactor of Greenfield School.*
Bottom: *Greenfield boys playing cricket in the park in the 1950s. This was before school uniform was readily available in the post-war years.*

In 1939 she had purchased Beechlands - the large Edwardian house in Brooklyn Road that is part of Greenfield today. During the war years, we know that Beechlands became a home for many of Ruth's relatives, three billeted Canadian officers, and a Russian emigré - complete with parrot! Ruth resigned her teaching post in 1947 to care for a sick friend who subsequently died, thus when the offer of Greenfield was made in 1948 she was more than ready to take it on.

Joyce Pearce lived in Woking and went up to Oxford in 1933 to read history at Lady Margaret Hall; she subsequently became senior history teacher at Mitchum Girls' School. Together with a friend she met there - Margaret Dixon - she organised weekend discussion groups for sixth formers in her home in Streatham. After the war, her mother offered Joyce the use of Ockenden, a rambling

Above: Sports day, held at the Kingfield Football Ground in the 1950s. Top: The school's founders, Miss Ruth Hicks and Miss Joyce Pearce with girls outside the school at Constitution Hill in the 1950s. Right: 'Beechlands', home of Miss Ruth Hicks, which is now part of the school today.

house in White Rose Lane, and the weekend group discussions transferred to Woking. This was the somewhat unlikely genesis of what was to become a worldwide initiative, which still today assists refugees.

The legacy of Greenfield School enabled Ruth Hicks to take on a Headship, which she welcomed, whilst Joyce Pearce devoted herself to the ever-increasing demands of her Ockenden Venture as she called it. She was deemed to be the 'sleeping partner' of Greenfield, although she did teach some history. Allegedly she was a literal as well as a metaphorical sleeping partner and a story often repeated recounts how she would sometimes fall asleep during her history lessons. This came to light when a member of staff noticed girls tiptoeing out of a room; when questioned, the children explained that they 'did not want to disturb Miss Pearce!'

In the early days, the school had very basic resources. Ruth and Joyce believed in parsimony, re-cycling everything, even to the extent of placing staff wages - which were exceptionally low - into many-times used envelopes. By so doing, they were able to keep fees to an absolute minimum, making Greenfield accessible to more parents than might otherwise be able to afford an independent education for their children. Greenfield was very much a family school and there was no limit with regard to the number of children in each class. The school roll increased considerably in 1952 when children from refugee camps in Germany were brought to England through Joyce's Ockenden Venture and all became pupils at Greenfield. Many more were to follow, and a firm link between the two institutions was forged. Some twenty three years later, in 1975, with only three days warning, ninety nine small Vietnamese children arrived on a plane chartered by the Daily Mail, to be housed in Ockenden's homes, and continuing its long tradition, Greenfield helped to welcome them.

In 1954 Joyce's Ockenden Venture became a registered charity, and large numbers of her refugees were housed in Broken Hill, the impressive Edwardian house that sat exactly opposite Beechlands, another of Henry Quartermaine's properties, on the corner of Brooklyn Road. In the same year, as the number of pupils at Greenfield continued to increase, Ruth Hicks began converting rooms in Beechlands into classrooms for some of the senior girls. Eventually she gave over all but the attic, where she then lived. But it was less than satisfactory for girls to be continually walking between the two sites, so by the early 1970s the senior girls department was permanently

Top: *Greenfield children forming a nativity tableau behind Epworth Choir in the late 1970s.*
Above: *The junior school at Constitution Hill in the 1950s (now the Ockenden Venture).*
Right: *The school today.*

established in Beechlands; junior pupils remained at Constitution Hill and Ruth Hicks moved into Melbourne, a house which she had built in the grounds of Katana, the house opposite the school which was also part of the Quartermaine empire. At this point the name 'Beechlands' ceased to exist- both departments were called Greenfield School.

No school is complete without its nearby source of sweets and bottles of pop. How many ex-Greenfield pupils may remember where they got theirs? They may recall a Polish man called Chez by the pupils, who had survived one of the death camps, and came to England as a refugee. Chez ran the Claremont Stores - now the furnishing shop 'Are You Sitting Comfortably?' at the top of Blackness Lane, yards from the gates of Greenfield's junior department and this was the school's 'tuck shop' for many years.

Joyce Pearce died in 1985, Ruth Hicks the following year, and Greenfield acquired charitable status and a board of trustees. However, years of parsimony had taken its toll, and the buildings were in a very poor state, thus with the appointment of the present Bursar in 1988 - Linda Richardson - the trustees began what was to become an extensive building programme, over the next

en years. Sadly, it was clear by the end of 1991 that despite a new building, the senior girls' school was unlikely to be viable in the face of the abundance of other independent girls schools in the area. The trustees made the decision to close the senior school, move the junior department across to the Brooklyn Road site, and sell the Constitution Hill building. That they sold it to the Ockenden Venture seemed entirely right, reinforcing the association between the two establishments. Broken Hill was in its turn sold by the Ockenden Venture, and is now an apartment block, as is Katana and Melbourne, changing dramatically the face of this end of Brooklyn Road.

At the start of 1992 morale was low because of the impending closure of the senior department, the school was currently without a Head and numbers were beginning to fall. Facing the need for radical change, the trustees appointed the present Principal - Jennifer Becker - and the renaissance of Greenfield began.

Today, Greenfield bears little resemblance to its former self. Old Beechlands house is much extended, yet retains an Edwardian elegance. Still an independent co-ed school, now affiliated to the Incorporated Association of Preparatory Schools, it has an impressive library, ICT suite, spacious and colourful classrooms, purpose built sports hall, a lovely pavilion in landscaped grounds where once was the uncultivated garden of Ruth Hicks' home - and of course a website! Music plays an important part in school life, and Greenfield violinists, choirs, wind groups, orchestra and jazz group perform at the annual Woking Festival. Since 1960 Greenfield pupils have participated in the Epworth Christmas Concert, creating nativity tableaux, thus they celebrate the ruby anniversary of their first involvement in 2000.

However, some things never change, and Greenfield children can still be seen crossing the road at Constitution Hill to access Woking Park where they play football, cricket and hockey. Importantly, as well as having first class facilities and achieving excellent results, Greenfield remains a school with a sense of humour and a happy association with Woking town. School days should be purposeful but fun, memories should be happy ones, and that as much as anything is what Greenfield is about. Staff no longer receive scant pay in used envelopes - or fall asleep mid-lesson! Refugee pupils have long since gone, but we believe that despite sweeping changes, Ruth Hicks and Joyce Pearce would be very proud of Greenfield School today.

Above left: *Pupils in Woking Park with a performance poet in 1999.* ***Above right:*** *Children at play.* ***Left:*** *Children returning from a games lesson in the park. In the background to the left is the former junior school and to the right is the former Claremont Stores.*

Into space - under the sea

James Walker has been making seals and gaskets in Woking for nearly 75 years and has been a major employer in the town and at its height it employed over 2,000 at its Lion Works site. Today the James Walker Group is a dynamic manufacturing and distribution group with companies and links across the world and is an international force in the world of fluid sealing technology. Products bearing the James Walker name are used in virtually every major industry from the North Sea oil and gas industry to aerospace.

James Walker, a Scottish engineer, founded the company in London in the 1880s. After many years in the marine industry involved with seals and gaskets he succeeded in perfecting a high-pressure semi-metallic packing to cope with the then triple expansion marine engines. This new packing caused a revolution in the industry and was marketed under the soon famous Lion Brand. The names James Walker and Lion have been linked ever since and the poster from 1926 proudly claims that Lion Packing is the 'King of Packings'.

James Walker began manufacture in Poplar in the East End of London, in what would become the first Lion Works, employing six men and a boy. Business grew steadily and was soon filled to capacity with manufacturing plant specialising in high-pressure jointings, which quickly became standard equipment for ship builders, as well as rail and automobile engineers.

By 1926 the workforce had grown to 350 and had outgrown the London factory. More space was needed and the site at the corner of Oriental Road and Maybury Hill was bought, which became the Lion Works that so many residents in Woking remember.

The site had an interesting history before it was purchased by James Walker. The first buildings on the site were erected in 1860 as a Drama College and a home for retired actors with landscaped walks. The buildings then became the Oriental Institute, a centre for Oriental learning and the name of the nearby road was changed to Oriental Road. The Victorian building can be seen in the postcard of the Institute (below) taken about 1900.

Top left: *James Walker, founder of the company.*
Above right: *A poster from 1926.*
Below: *The Oriental Institute taken about 1900.*

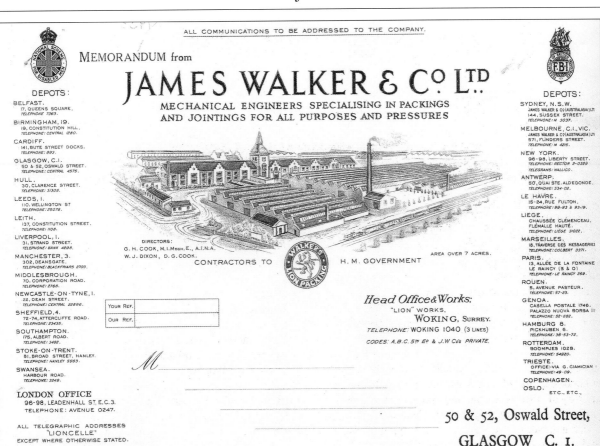

ALL COMMUNICATIONS TO BE ADDRESSED TO THE COMPANY.

MEMORANDUM from

JAMES WALKER & C° LTD.

MECHANICAL ENGINEERS SPECIALISING IN PACKINGS
AND JOINTINGS FOR ALL PURPOSES AND PRESSURES

DEPOTS:

BELFAST.
17, QUEENS SQUARE.
TELEPHONE 7363.

BIRMINGHAM, 19.
19, CONSTITUTION HILL.
TELEPHONE: CENTRAL 1280.

CARDIFF.
141, BUTE STREET DOCKS.
TELEPHONE: 893.

GLASGOW, C.I.
50 & 52, OSWALD STREET.
TELEPHONE: CENTRAL 4575.

HULL.
30, CLARENCE STREET.
TELEPHONE: 31305.

LEEDS, I.
110, WELLINGTON ST
TELEPHONE: 25078.

LEITH.
137, CONSTITUTION STREET.
TELEPHONE: 1108.

LIVERPOOL, I.
31, STRAND STREET.
TELEPHONE: BANK 4295.

MANCHESTER, 3.
302, DEANSGATE.
TELEPHONE: BLACKFRIARS 2703.

MIDDLESBROUGH.
70, CORPORATION ROAD.
TELEPHONE: 2766.

NEWCASTLE-ON-TYNE, I.
22, DEAN STREET.
TELEPHONE: CENTRAL 22896.

SHEFFIELD, 4.
72-74, ATTERCLIFFE ROAD.
TELEPHONE: 23435.

SOUTHAMPTON.
175, ALBERT ROAD.
TELEPHONE: 3482.

STOKE-ON-TRENT.
81, BROAD STREET, HANLEY.
TELEPHONE: HANLEY 5863.

SWANSEA.
HARBOUR ROAD.
TELEPHONE: 3249.

LONDON OFFICE
96-98, LEADENHALL ST, E.C.3.
TELEPHONE: AVENUE 0247.

ALL TELEGRAPHIC ADDRESSES
"LIONCELLE"
EXCEPT WHERE OTHERWISE STATED.

DIRECTORS:
G. H. COOK, M.I.MECH.E., A.I.N.A.
W. J. DIXON, D. G. COOK.

CONTRACTORS TO   H. M. GOVERNMENT

AREA OVER 7 ACRES.

Head Office & Works:
"LION" WORKS,
WOKING, SURREY.
TELEPHONE: WOKING 1040 (3 LINES)
CODES: A.B.C. 5TH E° & J.W C°'s PRIVATE.

YOUR REF.
OUR REF.

DEPOTS:

SYDNEY, N.S.W.
JAMES WALKER & C° (AUSTRALASIA) LTª
144, SUSSEX STREET.
TELEPHONE: M 3037.

MELBOURNE, C.I., VIC.
JAMES WALKER & C° (AUSTRALASIA) LTª
571, FLINDERS STREET.
TELEPHONE: M 4215.

NEW YORK.
96-98, LIBERTY STREET.
TELEPHONE: RECTOR 2-0389
TELEGRAMS: WALLICO.

ANTWERP.
50, QUAI STE. ALDEGONDE.
TELEPHONE: 334-02.

LE HAVRE.
15-24, RUE FULTON.
TELEPHONE: 99-93 & 93-19.

LIÈGE.
CHAUSSÉE CLÉMENCEAU.
FLEMALLE HAUTE.
TELEPHONE: LIÈGE 31022.

MARSEILLES.
18, TRAVERSE DES MESSAGERIES
TELEPHONE: COLBERT 3371.

PARIS.
13, ALLÉE DE LA FONTAINE
LE RAINCY (S & O)
TELEPHONE: LE RAINCY 259.

ROUEN.
5, AVENUE PASTEUR.
TELEPHONE: 57-23.

GENOA.
CASELLA POSTALE 1746.
PALAZZO NUOVA BORSA II
TELEPHONE: 52-662.

HAMBURG 8.
PICKHUBEN 6.
TELEPHONE: 36-53-72.

ROTTERDAM.
BOOMPJES 102B.
TELEPHONE: 54920.

TRIESTE.
OFFICE: VIA G. CIAMICIAN
TELEPHONE: 49-09.

COPENHAGEN.

OSLO.
ETC., ETC.,

50 & 52, Oswald Street,
GLASGOW C. I.

The notepaper (above) from the 1930s shows an artist's impression of the early Lion Works factory. By this time James Walker had already built up an extensive network of offices at home and overseas.

Many residents of Woking will remember driving under the railway bridge on Maybury Hill with its distinctive sign informing drivers that they were approaching James Walker's Lion Works.

As can be seen from the aerial photograph of Lion Works taken in the mid 1960s (overleaf) almost every inch of the site was covered by factory and office buildings. Because the site was so large and so many people were employed there, James Walker had its own fire service and many other support services such as a canteen, social club and welfare department.

In 1908 the site was sold to Martinsyde Ltd who retained the original building and built their early factory in the grounds for the manufacture of aeroplanes. Between 1910 and 1918 the company was the third largest aircraft manufacturer in this country. Martinsyde began making motorcycles in 1922 and some 2,000 motorcycles were built, of which about 20 remain today. Due to a general slump in the industry the site was put up for sale.

On its acquisition in 1926, James Walker moved all its manufacturing from London to Woking and continued to develop the Lion Works Site.

Top: *The 1930s letterheading, showing the Lion Works.*
Above: *The Lion Works Fire Service.*
Right: *The bridge sign in the 1960s.*

Because of continued business expansion James Walker bought a green field site in Old Woking in 1960 on which it built the Hoe Bridge factory. Today this is James Walker's main factory in Woking employing 280 people.

The Lion Works site was sold in the mid 1990s and is now the Lion Retail Park. However, the links

forged nearly 75 years ago with the site are still strong in that Lion House, part of the old Lion Works site, now houses the International Headquarters of the James Walker Group.

James Walker's world-wide reputation for excellence in fluid sealing over the last 75 years owes so much to the skill and commitment of the thousands of employees who have and who still work for the Company at its factories and offices in Woking. Many employees have achieved 40 years' faithful service to the Company. Fathers and sons, mothers and daughters, brothers and sisters have all worked for the Company and the Lion Works has seen many a romance blossom.

The inventiveness shown by Mr Walker has been continued by others throughout the years. The Company is still at the forefront of fluid seal development and materials science to provide industries worldwide with top quality products that are vital to the safe and efficient operation of plant and machinery. James Walker manufactures over 250,000 different fluid sealing products: gaskets, compression packings and seals of virtually every size and industry standard. Over three million items are held for immediate despatch through automated distribution centres and a global network of James Walker companies and distributors.

Left: *The company's products today.*
Above: *An aeriel view of Lion Works.*

A picture of progress

Woking's longest established photographic dealer was founded in the 1920s by George Harper, an optician who opened his first shop at 29 Guildford Road. By 1930 Harpers had begun selling photographic equipment.

In the mid 1930s Harpers moved into Woking's main shopping street, then called Commercial Road, allowing the photographic side of the business to expand. During the second world war George Harper even employed staff to handle the developing of films for the local military base at Pirbright.

George Harper continued to run the business until his retirement in 1962. The firm was then sold to John Symonds, a commercial photographer. John continued to build the photographic side of the business employing a full time photographer to assist him. Many local and national firms benefited from his expertise which included making industrial movies for showing at exhibitions long before the days of video.

In 1969 Martyn Rees joined John working part time as an industrial photographer. By 1974 Martyn had moved full time into the retail side of the business and become a director of the company.

Harpers doubled in size in 1979 when adjacent premises became available. There Harpers became one of the first local companies to sell computers, becoming one of the top dealers in Amstrad PCs under the management of Simon Pilsworth.

From 1984 Martyn Rees and his wife Ann became part owners of Harpers and in 1990 they took full control.

From the start of the 1980s Harpers had started to build a reputation as major suppliers of audio visual (AV) and presentation equipment. In 1987 Harpers AV Ltd under Ken Foster MD moved into specially converted premises in Old Woking. That move enabled a rapid expansion into the field of video editing and production as well as a large hire and conference department which now operates from premises on the Woking Business Park.

After more than 20 years in the same retail premises Harpers' shop later moved to 59-61 Commercial Way. Here Harpers became amongst the first in the country to install machines capable of producing high quality prints from both traditional film and digital media - a long way from the box Brownies of the 1920s!

Below: *Harper's today.*
Bottom: *Harper's in 1963.*

Setting types for model printers

For 150 years and over five generations Unwins have made their living by the printed word, ten of them in printing and four in publishing. Today the family business is in the control of others but their involvement with the printed word continues. The Unwins' story is a fascinating one however, not least the part which took place in the Woking area.

The saga began with the enterprise of Jacob Unwin, (1802-1855) who became apprenticed in 1816 to a small printer in the City of London. Within three years of completing his apprenticeship he acquired a little printing office with a single hand press and one journeyman and so started the business which grew over the years into the Gresham Steam Press, and under his sons George and Edward into Unwin Brothers of London and Woking. George was the head of the firm from 1855 until the limited company was formed in 1902 when he became the Senior Director. The London works, which in the 1890s poured out 300,000 copies a month of the famous 'Strand', and also other popular magazines, was obliged to close down during the first world war.

Afterwards, under George Soundy Unwin (the third generation in the business), the Woking endeavour which had begun in 1896, was built up through the 1920s into one of the largest units of Monotype composition in the south of England, producing hundreds of books for leading publishers and many magazines and scientific periodicals.

It was a fire in the firm's plant at Chilworth which necessitated a new site be found for the establishment of an alternative printing works. The task fell to

Above left: *George Unwim.*
Below: *The composing room at Pilgrim Street.*
Bottom: *One of the firm's earliest methods of transport*

...eorge Soundy Unwin who was 27 at the time and he ...sponded well to the challenge that faced him. The ...mily had experience of using water power and ...ough it was by no means essential to rely on this ...wer, the family was in favour of it and George was ...ven the commission of finding it in West Surrey, with ...d speed. On foot, by bicycle and in hired horse-drawn ...aps George Soundy, scoured the area throughout the ...inter of 1895-1896. After several abortive journeys ...e old disused paper mill lying across the River Wey ... Old Woking, to the south of the railway was ...iscovered and quickly decided upon.

...here had been flour mills, latterly paper mills at that ...oint for 900 years. It was the insistence of George ...oundy's father, George Senior that a decent architect ...e commissioned to design the necessary alterations to ...e mill which resulted in the handsome new facade ...uilt in the Flemish style in warm red brick.

...bove: Woking Works c1925.
...op: The heyday of hot-metal setting.

Working hours at that time were 7 a m to 6 p m Mondays to Fridays and till 12 noon on Saturdays, a fairly standard working week in those days. In the early years of the 20th century the Woking plant was a thriving concern and the spirit of the staff was essentially good and a high quality of book-work was produced.

The second world war brought problems to the firm, not least the shortage of labour, paper and even machinery. Additionally, Unwins, in common with most others were quite unprepared for the steep rise in all of their costs, due to inflation. In addition to this the family was under constant threat that their Woking premises would be commandeered for use in wartime aircraft production, something which fortunately never came to pass.

From conventional hot metal and letterpress printing, the firm moved boldly on in the 1950s and 1960s under Rolf (of the fourth generation) and his sons, to the technical revolution of 'cold setting' - first by specially adapted IBM typewriters, then photo-composition and the computer.

The 1960s saw the firm move out of independent family control when it was purchased by the Staples Printing Group. The assets of the firm by that time included a well-equipped printing plant of a complexity and capability that would have astonished an earlier generation. However a far more valuable asset is the expertise which the Unwin family were able to bring to the new company, a cumulation of several lifetimes of experience in the printing business which continues to this day.

How does your garden grow?

'**P**arsley, sage, rosemary and thyme' go the words of the song. It's strange how one only needs to say those words to smell the rich aroma of our favourite herb. Herbs have been valued for hundreds (even thousands) of years, not only being used to add their delicious flavour to our food but also as an essential source of health giving tonics and medicine. But where do the herbs we buy today come from?

A great many of them come from the well known Woking firm of herb growers R&G Stevens founded in 1958 by Richard and Gloria Stevens. Today the firm employs almost a hundred staff and is one of the largest specialist cut herb producers in the United Kingdom. Before the husband and wife team embarked upon their joint enterprise Richard 'Steve' Stevens had worked as a salesman at the old Covent Garden market and been inspired to start producing his own herbs for sale. The couple slowly but surely built up a reputation for the freshness, flavour and natural goodness of their herbs as

well as the quality of the service they offered customers with a working ethos of never putting anything in a packet they would not buy themselves, and never putting underneath what they wouldn't put on top.

The business actually began in the Stevens' back garden in Ottershaw in Surrey with Gloria packing the products whilst, using only ordinary garden hand tools, Richard grew and sold the herbs. The demand increased and when the back garden could no longer cope a neighbour grew more for them. Richard meanwhile kept up his full time job until he left to run the business full time in 1973, by which time Gloria was running packing department with ten women and schoolboys doing weekend and evening shifts.

Three years earlier the Stevens' had however already moved to the present larger premises, Lucas Green Nurseries in

Above: *Planting by hand.*
Below: *The premises from the air.*

cooking inspired by the seemingly endless free publicity given by TV chefs who invariably exhort their audience to buy fresh rather than dried herbs. Another important area of business growth has been an ever increasing interest in ethnic foods and vegetarian dishes, of which herbs are often an integral part.

To ensure year round supplies, the business imports herbs from Mediterranean countries (Spain, Italy, Israel and Cyprus), North Africa and the Far East. From their modern packing operation about 140,000 consumer units and catering packs per week are distributed to supermarkets, caterers and retail outlets.

The Stevens retired in 1990 and were followed in the business by their daughter Jennie Prestwich her husband Warren and now, the third generation, the Stevens' grandson Mathew. Fresh herbs are now a multi-million pound business rather than a cottage enterprise, and the Prestwich family are very much at the centre of that industry. R&G Stevens continues to seize the opportunities and rise to the challenges of the unique market in fresh herbs.

The next time we are in a restaurant eating a deliciously prepared meal or browsing the supermarket shelves looking for herbs we may pause to recall that the chances are high that our ultimate enjoyment will in large part be down to the hard work and dedication put in by this firm's founders, Richard and Gloria Stevens.

oking's West End. The house and five acres of eglected nursery land presented a real challenge, earing the ground of endless weeds and preparing the il for growing.

eeding in the herb business is much harder than non-ardeners might imagine: herbs are very easily damaged y weed killers and as a result much of the weeding had to e done by hand - a real labour of love!

he old hand tools were retired eventually to be replaced y tractors, cultivators, greenhouses and modern spraying quipment. The main market has now switched from old ovent Garden to the New Covent Garden market where e firm has two stands, the main customers being retailers nd catering suppliers.

emand for fresh herbs has continued to grow, fuelled part by ever more discerning and adventurous

op left and right: The premises.
bove: *Exhibiting at the Festival of Food and arming.* **Right:** *Gloria and Richard Stevens.*

Accounting to the highest level

A firm of accountants which has been a well-respected presence in Woking for the best part of the last century traces its origins to one man who earned the trust of many local small businesses which put their accounting affairs into his hands. The practice is starting the new century fully equipped to handle the increasingly complex financial matters in today's business world while still holding on to the integrity and principles of its founder.

Herbert Parnell qualified as an Accountant whilst working as a Woking Council Officer. During the evenings he used his accounting skills, to act on behalf of several small businesses . This activity gradually became more demanding on his time, to the extent that it soon became viable for him to set up his own accountancy firm. This he did in 1920.

He was a sole practitioner for 25 years, working from premises in 2 High Street, Woking, when in 1945 J T Risbridger joined from a Guildford firm; 'J T' as he was known, was a practising member of the Chartered Institute of Certifed Accountants for 50 years.

As the number of clients expanded so did the number of staff required to do all the necessary work, and larger premises were sought. The practic acquired additional premises down the road to 22 High Street in 1958. Some years later, in 1971 any frustrations involved in running a practice from tw locations came to an end when the firm transferred all operations to 136 Kingsway, Woking, a short walk away from their present offices at Kingsway House, Goldsworth Road.

The expertise in commercial accounting really began in the mid 1970s when a former Finance Director joined as a Partner, and the present team of accountants started to be assembled in the late 1970s when Alan Hodgetts and Richard Barwick joined from City firms.

Above: *Founder, Herbert Parnell.*
Below: *The firm's office at 123 Kingsway, Woking.*

small local businesses which had been the foundation business of Herbert Parnell's original venture.

Obviously the traditional Accountancy services form the basis of the company's work, but now they are extending their involvement with clients working closely with the development of each business. In many cases the Partners are acting as Financial Directors for clients together with other roles traditionally completed within the client companies such as payroll, outsourced management accounting marketing - all functions which allow the client to concentrate on what they are good at and letting Herbert Parnell do the rest.

This means that the staff at today's Herbert Parnell have to possess a multitude of skills, including different languages such as German, French, Italian, Greek and even Armenian!

Herbert would also not recognise the internet and its application for business. The company's website, www.herbertparnell.com, advertises the firm's services to the world and offers help and advice, and with an increasing number of international companies as clients the internet is used for data transmission and to embed the firm's services with the client's business.

Herbert Parnell was a forward thinking active member of the Woking Chamber of Trade and Commerce, holding the office of President from 1935-36. The firm has maintained links with the Chamber, still taking an active interest in their affairs, and the current Managing Partner John Flewitt has followed in the founder's footsteps, having also served as President during 1999/2000. He was actively involved in raising money for the purchase of heart defibrillators for use in public places within Woking. One particularly successful fund-raising event involved abseiling down the side of an office building. Other members of the Herbert Parnell staff joined in and a great deal of money was raised *(above)*.

There are now many areas of work the firm is involved in that Herbert would not recognise. John Flewitt joined in 1984 and together with partners Andrew Hodgetts and Adrian Peckham, are transforming the firm, with clients ranging from UK subsidiaries of internationally known companies to

However, this does not mean that Herbert Parnell are moving away from their established client base, some of whom have been with the firm for over 50 years. The firm continues an important tradition established by its founder, namely that the partners and other staff work according to Christian principles. It is part of the commitment they make to each client that they 'will act with integrity, honesty and openness'.

Another important factor within the company is fun - perhaps a little surprising in the light of the conventional view of accountants - the partners and staff believe in making work enjoyable and regularly do out of work activities together including - potholing, go-karting, quiz nights, trips to France, weekends away and bowling.

Above: *Abseiling down the side of an office building for fund-raising.*
Right: *Today's partners: John Flewitt (top), Adrian Peckham (bottom left) and Andrew Hodgetts.*

BBF Fielding - building connections in Woking

The profession of architecture has a long and noble tradition. Architects armed with set squares, measuring sticks and building plans drawn on paper, or rather papyrus, were already recognised at the time the Pyramids were built thousands of years ago. Since then the profession has been responsible not only for the other six wonders of the ancient world but the countless architectural marvels of the modern one.

One local firm of architects, Woking's BBF Fielding Ltd, is the proud inheritor of that ancient tradition.

The company was founded in 1962 by Maurice C Fielding, an architect who had previously worked for the Ministry of Public Building and Works before branching out on his own.

Maurice Fielding initially began working from his own home, later taking offices in Addlestone before finally moving in 1965 to the firm's current offices in Fielding House, a converted grain warehouse at 41 Chobham Road, Woking.

The young firm began life as a simple, straight-forward architect's practice; since then however its scope has expanded and today services include structural engineering, planning super-vision, building surveying, property services and project management.

Maurice's son Anthony joined the growing practice of ML Fielding and Associates in 1972. Anthony Fielding is still a director of the current company.

It is easy to look back and see an unbroken line of success and triumph; but such a rosy view would be deceptive. Building any business is never easy. And achieving long term success in the building industry is particularly difficult. The practice has survived the various recessions which always hit the building industry first and worst, and which are so often the barometer of the whole economy. Resilience, expertise, a fine reputation and the will to weather the multiple economic storms ensured that unlike many competitors ML Fielding and Associates was able to survive where less able and less adept contemporaries disappeared.

Today the firm's main market is in the commercial world, with framework agreements for such clients as British Telecom, the Post Office and the Inland Revenue. In addition the firm also works regularly for Local Authorities, Hospitals and many other public bodies. The practice also carries out residential, industrial, leisure and historical work including individual commissions and extensions. The practice has even gone international in association with a Belgian Architect and has been involved in projects in Bruges and Ghent.

The firm believes that its main selling points and attributes, which will ensure its continuing progress, are consistently forging good relation-ships with clients, delivering their product on time, within budget and to specification.

ML Fielding and Associates, the original partnership, became a limited company in 1996. The company merged with another practice, the BBF Consultancy Group, to become BBF Fielding Ltd on 1st June 2000. The new

Above: *Maurice Fielding, founder of the company.*

Every architect can take pride in belonging to a profession which has done more than most to shape our country

The link with Woking was enhanced by the company merger and by the appointment of Ray Freeland, a former Chief Architect of Woking Borough Council, as a director.

Looking to the future as well as to the past the practice encourages people who wish to pursue a career in architecture by providing placements for work experience and for graduate architect students.

Trends in building styles and materials change continually as a result of fashion and of technology. From the modernist style of the 1960s to the current emphasis on environmental harmony architects must keep abreast of public taste and need.

Architecture is a profession which literally charts the history of our towns. Buildings are themselves permanent monuments to those who use their expertise to provide us with our houses, offices, shops and factories.

Not every architect may have the privilege of designing a pyramid, but every a architect can take satisfaction in belonging to a profession which has done more than any other to shape our country - an environment which our ancestors would regard as a very real wonder of the world.

ompany plans to continue to expand and onsolidate its success.

he practice seeks to maintain strong links with he local community and enjoys a long-standing vorking relationship with many local clients ncluding the Borough Council. It has been nvolved with numerous development schemes n the area and has experience of the impor-ance of public consultation in town planning nd on architectural matters.

Below: One of the firm's recent local contracts.

Not so foolhardy as it seemed

It was an April Fool's Day decision that gave birth to the publication that has endured 78 years in the life of Woking and has been an integral part of the community.

It was in 1924 at the 1 April meeting of Woking Chamber of Trade, that G Langford, seconded by S Bailey, proposed that the Chamber adopt a magazine to encourage local shopping. It was unanimously carried.

On Thursday, 8 May that year, the Chamber launched 'Woking Offers' with a view to encouraging local trade and making traders' views known to the town's population.

This served them well for nearly ten years, then a change of title was considered and adopted. The publication became the 'Woking Review' in 1933 and through its columns the original aims are still maintained.

The distribution figure for the first issue was 5,000. Today the 'Review' has a distribution of almost ten times that number and is received in homes, offices and organisations throughout the borough and beyond.

It was profitable from its first issue and after six months F W Cooke of Sports House, Woking announced that it had paid its way. The success had been forecast by Sir William Perring, National Chamber of Trade president, who had said 'The finest thing for any town to do was to run its own newspaper or magazine in co-operative fashion'.

By January 1925, 'Woking Offers' had been handed over to H Clayton to publish under the auspices of the Chamber. In 1928 Mr Clayton changed the name to 'Woking Outlook' and Knight and Sons of Goldsworth Road, was the printer Arthur V Hills became the publisher and changed the name to 'Woking Review'.

The 'Woking Review' passed through several hands before becoming part of the Surrey Advertiser Group in 1976, and, more recently, Surrey and Berkshire Newspapers Ltd, part of the regional newspaper division of Guardian Media Group plc.

In the early years the publication championed causes, encouraged reader participation and maintained a lively link between townspeople, council and trading community. Over the years the 'Review'; has continued to publicise town activities, explain traffic and planning ideas, support events, keep residents informed of local issues affecting them and provide an outlet for townspeople's views and opinions

The 'Woking Review' sponsors sporting and leisure events and has its own Invitation Evening Cricket League, launched in 1935 a Review Bowls Trophy competition, launched in 1937 and Review Bowls Flitch competition (1982). The newspaper sponsors short-mat bowls, junior angling matches, a Junior Red Cross award, Star Discoveries talent shows, shop window competitions, a children's portrait contest and Woking in Bloom, which followed the Woking Floral Challenge launched by the 'Review' in the 1980s in conjunction with the Chamber

Top left: *Arthur V Hills, first publisher of The Review.*
Above centre: *Three early editions of the paper.*

of Trade. The 'Review' provides trophies for local events and publishes competitions that provide thousands of prizes for readers.

With the 'Addlestone and Byfleet Review', launched in 1933 for Byfleet, West Byfleet, New Haw, Addlestone, Rowtown, Ottershaw and the outlying areas, it is distributed to the major part of Woking Borough as well as parts of the boroughs of Runnymede and Surrey Heath.

The Review's 'Property Weekly' offers a 24 - 32 page notice board for local property and is used by all the main estate agents for providing details of properties for house buyers and sellers and the letting and renting sector and is eagerly awaited each week by those wanting to move house.

Although part of a large newspaper group, the 'Review', under its present editor and management team, maintains its independence and jealously guards its reputation for accuracy, credibility and readability.

The 'Review' is a reliable source of information on local government issues, police news, social club activities, sport, arts, motoring news and entertainment and continues to provide a newspaper market place for the town's goods and services, and as such provides a valuable contribution to the local community.

The 'Woking Review' today is a healthy, mature newspaper and boasts of being Woking's most widely read newspaper and the oldest free newspaper in the country.

Top left: *School children visiting the Review c1985.*
Top right: *Review Top Tot competition. First winner, Fiona Grundy in 1981.* **Below:** *Review Star Discoveries talent shows: former Review staff with 1987 winner Sarah Winbourne and Ray Alan and David Lodge.*

Hot off the press

The first issue of "The Woking News" hit the streets on October 19 1894 and proudly laid out its editorial policy. "First in regard to party politics, we want to take our neighbours into our confidence. To pose as the arbiters of public rights and wrongs, so far as national politics are concerned, it is not the goal towards we set our face. We will be neither Conservative nor Liberal, but will assume and maintain an attitude of perfect independence in reference to these opposing methods and parties in the State.

"Now everybody will run away with the idea that because we do not take up with a particular party, we are therefore, and necessarily without political principal, or that we have no moral backbone. In rebuking an error where we find it, we trust to be always in the forefront, but with 'party' we will have nothing to do; we cater for the people as a whole, irrespective of their opinions; to give news, to supply information, to keep our readers well posted up in all matters connected with the district, and to afford space for the ventilation of matters concerning anything of local interest is, at present what we aspire to."

Those aspirations, and the political policy, outlined by publisher Mr W. Moore in his first issue, costing one penny and produced from offices in Chertsey Road, have served the paper well for more than 100 years. Mr Moore, who ran a stationery business, referred to the impending changes in local government, which is why the Woking Borough Council celebrated its centenary alongside the paper in 1994. He promised his new reader: "The meetings of the Local Borough, soon to change its name and probably its personnel, will be fully reported, and, where possible, discussions as to its proceedings will be invited through our columns. "A vast work has to be performed by our local authority, and it is right that a watchful eye should be kept upon their doings, and that the electorate should have an opportunity of seeing how far the pledges made on the platform are kept in the Board Room."

Mr Moore extolled the virtues of his new publication as an advertising medium. "To the local trader, whose goods will be thus brought before every class of the community, the opportunity of making known his business, his wares and his prices which the Woking News presents, is exceptional to outsiders, who wish to influence local interests, our columns afford a splendid scope of usefulness, and to every class of advertiser the fact of a paper such as ours, possessing such facilities and circulation over the whole neighbourhood taking with it the information they seek to convey to every one of the inhabitants, will commend itself to their judgement as being one of the best means of publicity they could adopt." That is just as true of today's paper, but the sentences are shorter!

Mr Moore ended his first editorial with the entreaty: "If each reader will buy the Woking News regularly; make it his own by contributions of news as well as by the outlay of cash, this rapidly growing neighbourhood will be in the position which has long been its right, but which has been deferred until now, of having a paper that is a success, because of its news, its local character and its worth as a valuable advertiser.

The "News" certainly did prove a success, so much so that within a year it encountered competition. The first issue of "The Woking Mail" appeared on September 7, 1895. Its editorial trumpeted: "The Woking Mail is ushered into life today - the latest addition to the Press, the world's mightiest influence. We have been called into existence by the demands of a community already of the first importance as regards numbers, intelligence and wealth: and which is increasing with marvellous rapidity."

Messrs Chandler and Evans, of Goldsworth Road, under cut the "News" with their price of "one half penny", so more than a hundred years ago Woking experienced a price-cutting circulation battle that would have done Rupert Murdoch proud. In fact not only was the cover price halved, but copies of the first issue were given away free, as the underlined strap at the top of the first page said "With the proprietor's compliments."

It is not clear whether the "News" had carried advertisements which would have contravened today's

Above: *The issue dating from Friday, October 14, 1947.*

guidelines of having to be "legal, decent, honest and truthful," but the newcomers insisted that the "Mail" contained no "objectionable" advertisements. They boasted, using capital letters for emphasis: "Our sheet shall be fit for perusal by the most refined, and a Welcome Guest in every Home." They gave a clue to the possible objectionable material when they said: "No money lenders or quack advertisements will be inserted on any terms. The dignity of the Press includes responsibility, in a large measure, for the influence of published matter. We should not care to feel that we have been the means of assisting the sharks of Society to devour any of our readers who, in their innocence, believed the 'philanthropic' professions of these gentry."

Perhaps the "News" had also been too serious for some tastes, for the "Mail" promised to provide "something for everybody - informing, entertaining and suggesting." It remembered, somewhat sarcastically: "There are the womenfolk as the little ones, and for these and others who are not altogether absorbed in drainage schemes and fire escapes, we shall provide a compendium of the week's news - bright and brief."

In another apparent dig at the "News", the "Mail" said: "Notes on local and general topics will take the place of the usual long and dreary 'leading article' - though subjects of special importance will be treated at the length they deserve." The "Mail" also took a clear political stance, stating: "In politics we shall support

Above: *Floods which ravaged the area in September 1968.*

the Conservative party, from a firm conviction that it represents and converses the best interests of the Empire", but with the caveat: "Our local reports shall be impartial and without any offence to anyone." The new publisher added: One thing is certain - We have come to stay." At least, the paper had. In due course the Woodbridge Press has acquired the "Mail" from Chandler & Evans and then took over the "News", merging the papers into the Woking News and Mail.

The Woodbridge Press were owners until 1964 when the Woking News and Mail was bought by the Surrey Advertiser Group, which was then owned by families having a long connection with Surrey, whose managing director was Ray Tindle.
Under the Surrey Advertiser the Woking paper was part of a group which enjoyed a period of expansion when it became one of the largest independent newspaper organisations in the country. Then in 1979, 90% of the Surrey Advertiser Group was purchased by the Guardian and Manchester Evening News.

Sir Ray Tindle, who was knighted in the 1994 Queen's Birthday Honours for his services to the Newspaper Industry, retired from the board of the Surrey Advertiser Group in the autumn of 1997. Now wholly owned by the Guardian Media Group, the Woking News and Mail remains the biggest selling paper in Woking and now, as then, independence and local relevance are the key principles. Its move in 1999 to more modern offices in Poole Road, which it shares with sister paper the Woking Review, has strengthened its position as the prime record of the weekly news and events which form the pattern of Woking people's lives

A wonderfully nostalgic scene which was captured in Chertsey Road on VJ Day. Towns and cities all over the country put out the flags and prepared to celebrate as soon as they heard the news of the Japanese surrender on 14th August, 1945.

Acknowledgments

Patrick Evans

Trevor Fisher

Peter Sherwoood

Iain Wakeford, who edited the book

Penny Bray, editor of the Woking Review

Justine Stevenson, editor of the Woking News and Mail Series

Thanks are also due to
Peggy Burns and Margaret Wakefield who penned the editorial text
and Steve Ainsworth for his copywriting skills